GULSHAN I RAZ:

THE MYSTIC ROSE GARDEN

OF

SA'D UD DIN MAHMUD SHABISTARI.

THE PERSIAN TEXT, WITH AN ENGLISH TRANSLATION AND NOTES, CHIEFLY FROM THE COMMENTARY OF MUHAMMAD BIN YAHYA LAHIJI.

BY E. H. WHINFIELD, M.A.,
BARRISTER-AT-LAW,
LATE OF H. M. BENGAL CIVIL SERVICE.

London:
TRÜBNER & CO., LUDGATE HILL.
1880.

57

INTRODUCTION.

THE *Gulshan i Raz* was composed in A.H. 717 (A.D. 1317), in answer to fifteen questions on the doctrines of the Sufis, or Muhammadan Mystics, propounded by Amir Syad Hosaini,[1] a celebrated Sufi doctor of Herat. The author's name was Sa'd ud din Mahmud Shabistari, so called from his birth-place, Shabistar,[2] a village near Tabriz, in the province of Azarbaijan. From a brief notice of his life in the *Mujalis ul 'Ushshak*, repeated in substance in the *Haft Iklim*, the *Safina i Khushgu*, and the *Riaz ush Shu'ara*, it would appear that he was born about the middle of the seventh century of the Hejira (A.D. 1250), and that he died at Tabriz, where he had passed the greater part of his life, in A.H. 720. The only particulars of his life recorded in these *Tazkiras* are, that he was devotedly attached to one of his disciples named Shaikh Ibrahim, and that in addition to the *Gulshan i Raz* he wrote treatises entitled *Hakk ul Yakin* and *Risala i Shahid*. No further information as to the circumstances of his life and times is to be found in the poem itself or in the commentary, but we know from the *Habib us Siyar* and other chronicles[3] that his birth was about contemporaneous with the incursion of the heathen Moghuls under Hulaku Khan, the conquest of Persia, Syria and Mesopotamia, and the downfall of the Abbaside Khalifs, or "Vicars of God." And living as he did

[1] His life is given in the *Nafhat ul Uns* of Jami.

[2] This name is sometimes written Jabistar or Chabistar. The Persian *chim* is usually expressed by the Arabic *shin*.—Ouseley, Ibn Haukal, 156.

[3] See Malcolm, History of Persia, ii. 252.

at Tabriz, the capital of the newly established Moghul Empire, he must have witnessed the long struggle which ensued between the Christian Missionaries and the Muhammadan Mullas to gain the Moghul Sultans over to their respective religions,—a struggle the result of which was for a long time doubtful,[1] and which was not finally decided till A.H. 696, when the Emperor Ghazan Khan, with nearly one hundred thousand of his followers, adopted the Muhammadan faith. During the pendency of this struggle Tabriz was visited by missions from Pope Nicolas IV. and Pope Boniface VIII., and also by the celebrated Marco Polo; and possibly Mahmud's acquaintance with Christian doctrines may have been derived or improved from intercourse with Halton or some of the other monks attached to these missions.

The first European authors to notice the *Gulshan i Raz* were the travellers Chardin and Bernier, circ. 1700, both of whom describe it as the "Summa theologica" of the Sufis. In the course of the eighteenth century several copies of the poem found their way to the great European libraries. In 1821 Dr. Tholuck, of Berlin, published a few extracts from it, with Latin translations, in his "Ssufismus," and in 1825 a German translation of about one-third of the entire poem in his "Blüthensammlung aus der Morgenländischen Mystik." In 1838 Von Hammer-Purgstall published the Persian text, based on the Berlin and the Vienna MSS., along with a German verse translation and a few notes from Lahiji's commentary.[2] The text now published is based on that of Hammer, collated with two Indian MSS. of the poem and commentary,—one the poor copy in the library of the Asiatic Society at Calcutta, the other a very correct copy in the possession of a Zemindar in Midnapore. On the authority of this MS. several couplets omitted by Hammer have been restored, several repetitions retrenched, and

[1] One of the Moghul Emperors was actually baptised, and, according to the chronicler, "true believers trembled lest the sacred temple at Mecca might be converted into a Christian cathedral."—Malcolm, ii. 268.

[2] The full title of this commentary is, "*Mufatih ul a'jaz fi sharh i Gulshan i Raz.*" It was composed in A.H. 879.

various erroneous readings corrected.[1] All the alterations made have been indicated in the margin, and none have been made without MS. authority. Hammer's readings are marked H; those of the Midnapore MS., L.; and others, given in the commentary or in the Calcutta copy, MSS. The translation has been made as close to the original as possible, Lahiji's renderings, as given in his paraphrase, being strictly followed throughout. The translations of the Arabic quotations in the text are printed in italics. The notes contain a brief abstract of Lahiji's voluminous commentary, which is itself a great authority on Sufiism, and also a few of the more striking parallelisms to Sufi ideas to be found in the Neoplatonists, and in the mystical theologians of Europe.

It is this correspondence with European Mysticism which gives Sufiism its chief interest for European students. Many of the Catholic definitions of 'mystical theology' would do for descriptions of Sufiism.[2] The ruling ideas in both systems are very similar, if not absolutely identical. Thus, for instance, we find the Sufis talking of 'love to God,' of 'union with God,' of 'death to self, and life eternal in God,' of 'the indwelling in man of the Spirit,' of 'the nullity of works and ceremonies,' of 'grace and spiritual illumination,' and of the 'Logos.' Both systems may be characterised as religions of the heart, as opposed to formalism and ritualism. Both exalt the 'inner light'[3] at the expense of the outward ordinance and voice of the Church. Both exhibit the same craving for visionary raptures and supernatural exaltations, and have been productive of similar excesses and extravagancies. If Sufiism has its Mevlavis and Rafá'is and Beshara' fakirs, its dancing and howling, and Antinomian durveshes, so

[1] The poem is written in the metre called *Hazaj i musaddas i maksur*, viz. *mafá'ílun mafá'ílun mafá'íl* (twice).

[2] *E.g.* That of Corderius, "Sapientia experimentalis, divinitus infusa, quæ mentem ab omni inordinatione puram cum Deo intime conjungit." That of John a Jesu Maria, "Cœlestis quædam Dei notitia, per unionem voluntatis Deo adhærentis, elicita, vel lumine cœlitus immisso producta." That of Gerson, "Est motio anagogica in Deum—secretissima mentis cum Deo locutio."—Vaughan, i. 288.

[3] The Quaker Barclay, in his "Apology," supports his doctrine of "illumination" by reference to a Sufi book (the history of Hai Ibn Yokhdan) translated by Ockley.

European Mysticism has produced the Omphalopsychi or navelgazing monks of Mount Athos, the Jansenist "Convulsionaries," the Anabaptists of Munster, and the Shakers.[1] Finally, to complete the parallel, both systems have a tendency to Pantheism, and both use similar sensuous figures to express their visions and raptures. The Pantheism of the *Gulshan i Raz* has its counterpart in that of Eckart, the "Doctor Ecstaticus," and much of its sensuous imagery might be matched by the erotic language of St. Bernard's sermons on the Canticles, the wonderful effusions of St. Theresa, and the mystical hymns of St. Alphonso Liguori and others.[2]

At first sight it is difficult to see how a subjective emotional religious system like Sufiism could have originated from the rigid formalism of the Koran,[3] and still more how orthodox Mussulmans can possibly reconcile its Pantheism, as many of them do,[4] with the uncompromising Monotheism taught by Muhammad. The answer would seem to be that the Koran, and still more the *Hadis*, in one department of their language, contain the germs of this line of religious thought. They in fact use a double language. At one time they represent Allah as having created the world once for all, and as now removed to His seat in the *'arsh* or highest heaven, having left His creatures to work out their own salvation or condemnation by

[1] See an account of the curious phenomena which sometimes followed the preaching of Wesley, Whitfield, and Newton. Leslie Stephen's English Thought, ii. 417. And a missionary account of the "gracious visitations of the Holy Spirit at Vewa," one of the Fiji Islands. H. Spencer, Essays, i. 444.

[2] See Vaughan, "Hours with the Mystics," i. 119, ii. 125; and "Hymns and Verses of St. Alphonso," translated by Coffin, pp. 80 to 116.

[3] "Eam enim doctrinam ex arido atque exili Muhammadanismi solo tam cito esse enatam, res est per se admiratione digna, quæque desiderium illud menti humanæ ingenitum diserte attestatur, quo extra se proripitur et cum Deo rursus conjungi necessitate quadam naturæ vehementer cupit."—Dr. Pusey, in Nicoll's Catalogue of Bodleian MSS.

[4] The *Musnavi* is commonly said to be the Koran of Persia (Hughes, "Notes on Muhammadanism," p. 231); Khaja 'Ayni, an orthodox Sunni doctor, in a work published at Constantinople in 1834, warmly commends both the *Musnavi* and the *Gulshan i Raz*.—Hammer. Imam Shafei and Hanbal, two of the great jurisconsults, speak in the highest terms of the Sufis' "knowledge of God."—Tholuck, Ssufismus, 58.

their own free will, according to the lights given them by His prophets; at another time they represent Him as the 'Subtile' Being, immanent and ever working in His creatures, the sum of all existence, the 'fulness of life,' whereby all things move, act and exist, omnipresent, not only predestinating but actually originating all action, dwelling in and directly influencing and communing with each individual soul. The Sufis, being men of an emotional mystical temperament, or, as they called themselves, 'men of heart,' 'men looking behind the veil,' 'interior men,'[1] naturally caught at all expressions of this kind which seemed to bring the divine mysterious object of their religious emotion nearer to them, and, as theologians are prone to do, dwelt on the texts that fell in with their own view, to the exclusion of passages of the opposite tendency. This view they developed with the aid of the Greek and especially the Neoplatonic metaphysics, which had been popularised by the Arabian philosophers Farabi, Ghazzali, Ibn Roshd and Ibn Sina. Under these influences they identified the Allah of the Koran with the Neoplatonic Being, the One, the Necessary Being, the only Reality, "The Truth,"[2] the Infinite, which includes all actual being, good and evil, the First Cause, source of all action, good and evil alike. The world of phenomena and man—every thing else in fact but Allah—they identified with Not being,—absolute nonentity, which like a mirror reflects Being, and by thus borrowing particles of Being rises to the rank of Contingent being, a kind of being which, as Plato says, is and is not, and partakes both of existence and non-existence. This Not being is a sort of Manichæan Ahriman, which solves all practical difficulties attaching to their speculative system. According to their theory the Infinite includes all being, evil included; but as this is not consistent with the goodness of the Allah of the

[1] "While some (men of externals) believe that there is nothing in existence but what is visible to sight and reason, others (interior men) hold that much is veiled from sight which can only be seen through a nearer approach to the Divine Creator and a close spiritual communion with His omnipresent spirit."—*Fasus ul Hakim.*

[2] *Al Hakk*, das Seiende, the *Sat* of the Upanishads.—M. Müller, Upanishads, I., xxxii.

Koran, evil is said to proceed from Not being.[1] Again, according to their theory the spark of real being—divinæ particula auræ—in man is identical with the Infinite Being, and hence man would seem to be above laws and creeds; but as this would lead to Antinomianism, it is said that, while man remains in the intermediate state of Contingent being, he is as it were weighed down and held apart from Being by the element of Not being, and that in this probationary state laws and creeds are needed to restrain his evil tendencies. Thus, by the aid of this convenient 'Not being,' which is something while it is wanted, and relapses into nothing directly it is no longer needed, the Sufis avoid all the immoral and irreligious consequences of their theory.

Hence it is clear that the Pantheism of the Sufis, at any rate as expounded in the *Gulshan i Raz*, must not be confounded with the European Pantheism of the present day—that Pantheism which in the words of Bossuet, "makes every thing God except God himself." In the *Gulshan i Raz* we find a different species of Pantheism—one held conjointly with a theory of divine personality, and the obligations of morality. Mahmud's Pantheism is an amplification rather than a minimification of the idea of the Divinity, infinite, omnipresent and omnipotent.[2] He felt the sense of his own existence and his own freedom passing away and becoming absorbed in the sense of absolute dependence on this Infinite Being. Compared with this omnipresent, infinite, unseen Power underlying all the phenomena of the universe,[3] dominating man's will, striving in man's heart,—

> Warming in the sun, refreshing in the breeze,
> Glowing in the stars, and blossoming in the trees,—

all outward existences and agencies, whether in man or in the world,

[1] Similarly St. Augustine said evil was a negation. The fact that he could find no better way of reconciling these "antinomies of religious thought," ought to make us lenient critics of the Sufis.

[2] The same feeling is expressed by many Christian poets, *e.g.* Dante, Paradiso, iii. 86:

> "In la Sua volonta è nostra pace:
> Ella è quel mare, al qual tutto si muove,
> Ciò, ch' Ella cria, o che natura face."

[3] Mr. Herbert Spencer, "First Principles," p. 99, says: "We are obliged to regar

seemed to sink into utter nothingness. In point of fact Mahmud's Pantheism is only the corollary of the Muhammadan doctrine of *Jabr*, usually translated predestination, but, more exactly, the compulsion to carry out the Divine will, the universal action of Allah. The same sense and conviction of this irresistible divine impulse and compulsion which, according to their temperaments, drives some men into furious and fanatical action,[1] and makes others sit down and cry '*Kismat*,' impels men of a logical turn of mind to regard not only all the action but also all the existence in the universe as the direct outcome or manifestation of the Divine energy.

The whole Sufi system follows as a logical consequence from this fundamental assumption. Sense and reason cannot transcend phenomena, or see the real Being which underlies them all; so sense and reason must be ignored and superseded in favour of the 'inner light,' the inspiration or divine illumination in the heart, which is the only faculty whereby men perceive the Infinite. Thus enlightened, men see that the whole external phenomenal world, including man's 'self,' is an illusion, non-existent in itself, and, in so far as it is non-existent, evil, because a departure from the one real Being. Man's only duty is to shake off this illusion, this clog of Not being, to efface and die to self, and to be united with and live eternally in the one real Being—"The Truth." In this progress to union external observances and outward forms profit little, because they keep alive the illusion of duality, of man's self-righteousness, of his personal agency and personal merit, whereas the true course is to ignore all reference to self—to be passive, that God may work—and then the Divine light and grace will enter the chamber of man's heart and

every phenomenon as a manifestation of some power by which we are acted on, and though omnipresence is unthinkable, yet, as experience discloses no bounds to the diffusion of phenomena, we are unable to think of any limits to the diffusion of this power, while the criticisms of science teach us that this power is incomprehensible." Mahmud would agree that it is incomprehensible by reason, but would add that it is cognisable by spiritual illumination—the clairvoyance of the heart.

[1] Thus with us, the same theory of divine action upon the world which led the Puritans to action, led the Quakers to resignation, and 'quietism.' In popular parlance, "Quaker" signifies just the same sort of mild non-resisting character that "*Sufi Sahib*" does in India.

operate in him without impediment, and draw him to "The Truth," and unite him with "The One."

The manner in which these ruling ideas are worked out and connected, by means of allegorical interpretation, with the teaching of the Koran and the *Hadis* will be best explained by an outline of the poem.

After an exordium laying down the fundamental principle of the sole existence of the one real Being, and of the illusive non-real nature of all phenomenal being, and a short account of the composition of the poem, Mahmud proceeds to inquire how men are to gain this essential knowledge of God. The answer commonly given is, by thought. But thought is of two kinds, one logical reasoning, the other spiritual illumination. The first method is inapplicable, because sense and reason cannot transcend phenomena, and work up to the invisible and incomprehensible Being underlying them.[1] They are powerless to shake off the illusion of the apparent reality of the sensible world. From this original defect of mental eyesight, whatever philosophers and theologians say of God only proves their own incapacity to apprehend Him.[2]

II. Reason, looking at the Light of lights, is blinded by excess of light, like a bat by the sun. This annihilation of the mental vision caused by its proximity to the Light of lights—this consciousness of its own nothingness caused by its approach to Being—is the highest degree of perception which contingent being can attain.[3] When the contingent seer attains this state of annihilation of his phenomenal self, the true light is revealed to him, as a spiritual illumination streaming in on his soul.

The phenomenal world is in itself Not being, wherein are reflected, as in a mirror, the various attributes of Being. By a species of radiation or effluxion of waves of light from Being, each atom of Not being becomes a reflection of some one divine attribute. These

[1] Here is the germ of the modern doctrine of the Relativity of knowledge, and consequent limits of thought.

[2] Cognoscitur non secundum sui vim sed secundum cognoscentium facultatem.—Boethius. Hamilton, Metaphysics, i. 61.

[3] Compare St. Augustine: "Deum potius ignorantia quam scientia attingi."

effluent atoms of Being are ever striving to rejoin their source, but so long as their phenomenal extrusion lasts they are held back from reunion with their divine source.

Passing to precept, Mahmud says, "Rest not in the illusions of sense and reason, but abandon your 'natural realism,' as Abraham abandoned the worship of the host of heaven. Press on till, like Moses at Mount Sinai, you see the mount of your illusive phenomenal existence annihilated at the approach of Divine glory. Ascend like Muhammad to heaven, and behold the mighty signs of the Lord."

Thus illumined you will see "The Truth" to be the source of all being, diffused and poured out into the phenomenal world by means of the various emanations, beginning with the Logos and ending with man. "The Truth" it is who alone is acting in the universe. All the revolutions of the heavenly spheres, stars and planets, proceed not from themselves, as the undevout astronomer says, but from "The Truth." He is, as it were, the Master potter who turns the wheel. The motions of the heavens, the coalescence of discordant elements into bodies, the obedience of plants and animals to the laws of their kinds, are all His never ceasing handiwork.

With regard to man, he is the soul of the world—the microcosm. While other creatures reflect only single divine attributes, man reflects them all. He is an epitome of the universe, and so by introspection he may see in himself reflections of all the divine attributes—of the "fulness of the Godhead." But on the other side he is black with the darkness and evil of Not being. His object therefore should be to purge away this non-existent corrupt side of himself, which holds him back from union. And, union once attained, thought is no longer possible, for thought implies duality.

III. To "travel into self" means "introrsum ascendere,"—to journey out of the phenomenal non-existent self into the real self, which is one with "The Truth." This journey has two stages, dying to self and abiding in "The Truth." When man's phenomenal self is effaced, and the real Self alone remains, law has no longer any dominion over him.

IV. These journeys are called the "journey up to God" and the "journey down from God in God," and are a sort of circuit, and he who completes the circuit is the "perfect man."

When man is born into the world evil passions spring up in him, and if he gives way to them he is lost. But if he attends to the promptings of Divine grace and light in his soul, he repents, and is converted, and journeys up to God,—effacing self-will, self-knowledge, and his entire phenomenal corrupt self-existence; and purifying his nobler part from the stain of externality, he ascends in spirit to heaven, and is united in spirit with "The Truth."

This stage is the holy state known as saintship, exemplified in saints and prophets.

But the "perfect man" must not pause in this estatic union, which is above all laws. Notwithstanding this exaltation he must journey down again to the phenomenal world, in and along with God, and in this downward journey he must conform to outward laws and creeds. His sanctification must bring forth the outward fruit of good works.

The law is as a husk, and the holy state of identity with "The Truth" the kernel; and when the kernel is ripe it bursts the husk. But the perfect man must not rest or abide in this ecstatic state of union with "The Truth," but so long as he is in this life must "return to sobriety;" and though "The Truth" is the fixed and abiding home of his soul, he must wear the law as an outward garment, and the Sufi 'path' or canon as his inward garment, and perform all external legal observances.[1]

The perfection of this saintly state will be seen in Muhammad Mehdi, 'the seal of the saints,' who by the secret of unity will perfectly attain to "The Truth."

V. The man who knows this secret—that all things are One—dies to self, and lives, with regenerate heart, in God. He sweeps away all that comes between God and the soul, and "breaks through to the

[1] Another caution, insisted on as well by the Sufis as by European mystics, is that the vagaries of the "inner light" must be checked by recourse to the advice of the *Pir*, or "Spiritual Director."

oneness,"[1] as Eckart said. Good works, it is true, raise men to a 'laudable station,' but so long as division and duality and 'self' remain, true mystical union of knower and known is not attained.

VI. But if knower and Known be one, how comes it that the knower feels within him emotions of love and aspiration drawing him towards the 'Known?' In man's present phenomenal state, the mixture of Not being in him divides him from Being; and these aspirations are the stirrings of the true Being within him, recalling and drawing him as with a magnet to his source. If he be not of those who are born blind to this spiritual light within, these sparks kindle up the flame of love to God, which burns up his phenomenal self, and shows him his real self one with "The Truth."

VII. The man who, like Mansur Hallaj, the wool-carder, has carded away his phenomenal self, can say, "I am the Truth;" for when man takes his eternal side, 'other,' *i. e.* Not being, is annihilated, and nothing is left but Being. When God withdraws what belongs to Him all things fall back into their original nothingness. All phenomenal existence is merely an illusion, as we may see from the case of echoes, reflections, past and future time, and fleeting accidents, wherein all the externality or objectivity of substance consists.

VIII. The creature state being thus non-existent, man cannot of himself move, draw near to, or unite with "The Truth." Union is only a phrase for annihilating the phenomenal element in man—sweeping off the dust of contingent being. The genesis of the creature world is an eternal process. It is as a drop of water, raised from the sea of Being in mist, poured down in rain, converted into plants, animals, man, and finally recalled into the bosom of the sea. Phenomena are constantly annihilated in the universal Noumenon, and this annihilation is union.

[1] Similarly Tauler preached the necessity of "fathomless annihilation of self," and a "transformed condition of the soul," and "rest in the divine centre or ground of the soul."—Vaughan, i. 192.

IX. The illusion of free-will is Magianism, setting up an evil first cause, Ahriman, over against the good, Ormuzd. This illusion must be shaken off and annihilated in the conviction that the only free agent is "The Truth," and man a passive instrument in His hands, and absolutely dependent on His pleasure. Man's glory lies in abandoning his self-will, and finding his true will in God's will.

X. Going back to the relation of the law to the state of sanctification, called in the fourth answer "The Truth,"[1] and here called "the knowledge of faith," Mahmud compares the former to the shell, and the latter to the pearl within it. The Sufi must extract this pearl; but, on the other hand, he must not break the shell till the pearl within it is fully formed. The law is a schoolmaster to bring him to "The Truth." Without this faith, this fixed spiritual habitude, this settled internal character or 'state' of the heart, no external legal works are virtuous in the highest sense. Legal and formal works cannot sanctify man;[2] it is the saintly disposition which sanctifies works. From this disposition all the virtues flow spontaneously. All the virtues lie in the mean, in equipoise and harmony, and this harmony of the soul calls down and attracts the Spirit from above. This heavenly spirit operates in man like the sun's beams on the earth. As it were enamoured of the harmonious soul, the Spirit enters into a mystical marriage union with it, the issue of which is gracefulness, virtue and the beauty of holiness. But all these are not of man that worketh, but of God that giveth grace.

XI. Absolute Being is the *summum genus* embracing all being; but in one sense actual phenomenal being is wider, because it is absolute *plus* phenomenal limited being. This phenomenal side is

[1] Kashifi's abstract of the *Masnavi*, called *Lab ul labab*, arranges the matter of that poem under the three heads of the law, the path, and the truth.

[2] In the *Nafhat ul Uns*, the Shaikh of Islam is quoted as saying, "God is veiled from the heart of the man who relies on his own good works." Compare Luther's doctrine of justification by faith.

renewed every moment, as indicated by the texts about 'the new creation.' Similarly the texts about 'the resurrection and world to come' indicate that the dispositions acquired by men in this life will then be manifested in 'spiritual bodies,' *i.e.* forms appropriate to them. The perfect will then drink the 'pure wine' of union with God. There will remain no duality or distinction of persons. Hence faith, reason, devotion, paradise and *houris* will then become an empty tale.[1] Such will be the perfect 'union' in the world to come, but in this world all ecstatic union is followed by sobriety and separation.

XII. Mahmud concludes this part of the discussion by reiterating his main thesis that all things are One. The Eternal and the temporal are not two distinct entities, since the temporal is merely a subjective llusion, like the circle of fire seen when a single spark of fire is whirled quickly round.

XIII. to XV. These last three sections are devoted to an explanation of the figurative language whereby the Sufis express their onceptions of God and the universe, and their ecstatic experiences. And of this language it may be said that though it seems irreverent nd unseemly to us, it did not seem so to them. As Xenophanes[2] saw, men's conceptions of the Deity bear a constant relation to their wn moral and intellectual stature. Symbols that we see to be nadequate and misleading, were not improbably the highest attainable y the untutored minds of other ages and countries, and thus possessed, perhaps, a *relative* goodness of their own. Answer XV. shows us that one of the main characteristics of the Sufis was heir readiness to recognise and appreciate whatever seemed to them) be good and true in other religions, such as Christianity, Magianism,

[1] Law, author of the "Serious Call," got rid of gross material conceptions of eaven much in the same way.—L. Stephen, English Thought, ii. 407.

[2] Lewes, Hist. of Philosophy, i. 40.

and even Idolatry;[1] and there is high authority[2] (if authority be needed) for thinking it not inconsistent with our loyalty to our own religion to mete out similar tolerant measure to them.

[1] Dr. Wolff says of the Sufis of Bokhara, "They are people who really try, as they express themselves, to 'come nearer to God' by a moral life, separation from the world, meditation, prayer, *and reading the books of other religious sects*."—Missionary Tour, p. 205.

[2] *E. g.* The passage from St. Augustine quoted by Sale as the motto to his translation of the Koran—"Nulla falsa doctrina est quæ non aliquid veri permisceat;" and those from St. Augustine, St. Clement and others, quoted by Max Müller in the Preface to his "Chips."

ERRATA.

Page 26, note 5, line 3, *for* soul, *read* reason.
„ 31, note 2, line 5, *for* or, *read* and.
„ 40, note 3, line 1, *for* beholds, *read* beholds.
„ 41, couplet 409, *read* "The fourth is the purification of the secret from 'other.'"
„ 58, couplet 588, *erase* of.
„ 58, note 4, line 1, *erase* "or of the faith."
„ „ „ line 3, *insert* "or of the faith" *after* "knowledge of heart."
„ 62—3, note 8, *for* everything, *read* every action.

PERSIAN TEXT.

Title-page, line 2, *for* الملّه, *read* الملّة.
Couplet ٢٧٠, add in margin فرو ماندند L.
„ ٢١٠, *for* دحدت, *read* وحدت. This error of د for و occurs several times.

In the Name of God, the Merciful, the Compassionate.

EXORDIUM.

In the name of Him who taught the soul to think,
And kindled the heart's lamp with the light of soul;[1]
By Whose light the two worlds were illumined,
By Whose grace the dust of Adam bloomed with roses;
That Almighty one who in the twinkling of an eye,
From *Kaf* and *Nun* brought forth the two worlds![2]
What time the *Kaf* of His power breathed on the pen,[3]
It cast thousands of pictures on the page of Not being.
From that breath were produced the two worlds,[4]
From that breath proceeded the soul of Adam.
In Adam were manifested reason and discernment,
Whereby he perceived the principle of all things.
When he beheld himself a specific person,
He thought within himself "What am I?"[5]
From part to whole he made a transit,
And thence returned back to the world.
He saw that the world is an imaginary thing,
Like as one diffused through many numbers.[6]

[1] *I. e.* The reasonable soul, *nafsi natika.*

[2] *I. e.* The material visible world, and the invisible, spiritual or 'world of command.' ("Are not creation and command of Him?" Koran, *Sura* VII. 52.) The Sufis identified these with the Platonic worlds of ideals and of sensible objects. *Dabistan-i-Muzahib*, p. 445 (Calcutta edition).

[3] Pen (*kalam*) a name of *'Akl i kull*, universal reason, the first emanation from the "One." *Kaf*, *i. e. kudrat*, power. L.

[4] The command of God, *Kun fa-yakunu*, 'Be and it was,' is here alluded to. Koran, *Sura* II. 3. See Psalm xxxiii.. 9.

[5] See Milton's Paradise Lost, VIII. 270.

[6] The phenomenal world has no real 'objective' existence. It is only the repetition of the "One," (L.), who is, as Milton says:

. . . . . . Infinite
And through all numbers absolute, though One.
Paradise Lost, VIII. 420.

10 The worlds of command and of creatures proceed from one breath,
And the moment they come forth they go away again.
Albeit here there is no real coming and going,
Going, when you consider it, is naught but coming.[1]
Things revert to their proper original,
All are one, both the visible and the invisible.
God most high is the eternal one who with a breath
Originates and terminates both worlds.
The world of command and that of creatures are here one,
One becomes many and many few.
15 All these varied forms arise only from your fancy,
They are but one point revolving quickly in a circle.[2]
It is but one circular line from first to last
Whereon the creatures of this world are journeying;
On this road the prophets are as princes,
Guides, leaders and counsellors.
And of them our lord Muhammad is the chief,
At once the first and the last in this matter.
The One (*Ahad*) was made manifest in the *mim* of Ahmad.
In this circuit the first emanation became the last.[3]
20 A single *mim*[4] divides *Ahad* from Ahmad;
The world is immersed in that one *mim*.
In him is completed the end of this road,
In him is the station of the text '*I call to God*,'[5]

[1] See Answer XI. Coming and going are mere subjective impressions produced on the mind of the percipient by the rapid renewals of Divine manifestations. L.

[2] See Answer XII., *i. e.* the one Divine Being who is evolved, and rayed out through His various emanations down to man,—the lowest point in the circle,—and is united again to Himself in man's upward journey back to Unity. L.

[3] Ahmad, or Muhammad, is the type of the "perfect man," who is the theatre or exhibition place of all the Divine names and attributes. The first emanation, *'ayn*, was universal reason, and this descended, through the intermediate emanations, into man, and is again carried upwards by the "perfect man" in his ascent to "Unity," and is united with the "One." Thus the first becomes the last. L.

[4] *Mim*, the forty grades of emanations, from universal reason down to man. L.

[5] Koran, *Sura* XII. 108.

His entrancing state is the union of union,
His heart ravishing beauty the light of light.
He went before and all souls follow after
Grasping the skirts of his garment.
As for the saints on this road before and behind
They each give news of their own stages.
When they have reached their limits
They discourse of the 'knower' and the 'known,'[1]
One in the ocean of unity says '*I am the Truth*,'[2]
Another speaks of near, and far,[3] and the moving boat,
One, having acquired the external knowledge,
Gives news of the dry land of the shore.[4]
One takes out the pearl and it becomes a stumbling-block,
Another leaves the pearl and it remains in its shell.[5]
One tells openly this tale of part and of whole,[6]
Another takes his text from eternal and temporal:[7]
One tells of curl, of mole, and of eyebrow,[8]
And displays to view wine, lamp and beauty.[9]
One speaks of his own being and its illusion,[10]
Another is devoted to idols and the Magian girdle.[11]
Since the language of each is according to his degree of progress,
They are hard to be understood of the people.
He who is perplexed as to these mysteries
Is bound to learn their meaning.

[1] See Answer V.
[2] See Answer VII.
[3] See Answer IX.
[4] See Answer X.
[5] See Answer IV., Illustration 2. The positive law is the shell, and Sufi mysteries the pearl within it. One exposes these mysteries to the vulgar and causes scandal, another keeps them concealed. L.
[6] See Answer XI.
[7] See Answer XII.
[8] See Answer XIII.
[9] See Answer XIV.
[10] *I.e.*, of the illusive unreal nature of all phenomena, *ta'ayyunha*. L.
[11] See Answer XV.

THE CAUSE OF WRITING THIS BOOK.

Seven and ten years had passed after seven hundred,
From the Flight, when lo, in the month Shawál[1]
A messenger of a thousand graces and virtues
Arrived at the behest of the men of Khorásan.
A great man, who in that country is famed[2]
For his varied learning as a fount of light,—
Whom all the men of Khorásan, great and small,
Pronounce to be better than all men of this age,—
Had written an epistle on the matter of mystery
Addressed to the masters of mystery.
Therein many difficult expressions
In use amongst the masters of indications,
Had been versified in the form of several questions,
A world of mystery in a few words.
When the messenger read that epistle, forthwith
The news was noised abroad by many mouths.
All the nobles present in that congregation,
Turned their eyes upon this durvesh.
One who was a man well versed in affairs,[3]
And who had heard these mysteries from me a hundred times,
Said to me, "Tell the answers off straightway,
"That the men of the world may profit thereby."
I replied, "What need? for again and again
"Have I set forth these problems in treatises."
"True," said he, "but I hope to have from you
Answers in rhyme corresponding to these questions."

[1] 717 A.H.=1317 A.D.

[2] Amir Hosaini is the person referred to. See Introduction.

[3] Lahiji says the name of this person was Shaikh Aminuddin, and the conversation took place at Tabriz.

Wherefore at his solicitation I began
An answer to that epistle in concise terms.
Forthwith, in that illustrious congregation,
I pronounced this discourse without hesitation or repetition.
Now, with their wonted favour and kindness,
They will pardon my shortcomings;
All know that this person in his whole life
Has never attempted to write poetry.
And though his talents be competent thereto,
He has rarely had to compose verse.
Though he has composed many works in prose,
He has never compiled a *masnavi* in verse.
Prosody and rhyme weigh not mysteries,[1]
The pearl of mystery is not held in all vessels.
Mystery cannot be compressed into letters,
The Red Sea is not contained in a jug.
Why should I, to whom even words are lacking,
Why should I take on myself a further burden?
This is not boasting, but it is by way of compliment
And of apology to the men of heart.
I take no reproach to myself for my poor poetry,
For no poet like 'Attar is born in a hundred centuries.
Were there a hundred worlds of mystery set forth in this wise,
They would be only one grain from 'Attar's shop,[2]
But all this have I written of my own experience,
And not plagiarized as a demon from angels.[3]
In short, I delivered the answers to the questions
Off hand, each to each, neither more nor less.
The messenger took the letter with reverence,
And departed again by the road that he came.

[1] Prosody can "weigh" heavy and light (or, as we should say, long and short) syllables, but not Sufi mysteries. L.

[2] Fariduddin 'Attar, author of the *Mantik ut Tair*, &c., was a druggist.

[3] Koran, *Sura* XV. 18. The devils are said to ascend to overhear the talk of the angels in heaven.

Again that noble was instant with me,
Saying, "Do me yet another favour,
"Expound these mysteries which you have spoken.
"Out of theory bring them into evidence."[1]
I did not think it possible for me at that season
To treat thereof with the unction[2] of ecstasy,
For the explanation thereof in speech is impossible,[3]
The master of ecstasy alone knows what is ecstasy.
Nevertheless, according to the word of the teacher of the faith,
I rejected not the postulant of the faith,[4]
But to the end that these mysteries might be explained,
The parrot of my eloquence lifted up his voice.
By aid of heavenly grace and divine blessing
I spoke the whole discourse in a few hours.
When my heart craved of heaven a title for this book,
There came an answer to my heart, "It is our Rose Garden."
Since heaven has named it "Rose Garden,"
May it enlighten the eyes of all souls.

[1] From demonstrated knowledge, *'ilm ul yakin*, bring them to the stage of experienced or evidenced knowledge, *'ayn ul yakin*. The first is the knowledge gained by logical demonstration, the second that "spiritually discerned" by illumination, *Kashf*. L.

[2] *Zauk*, 'taste,' 'delight,' 'religious exaltation.'

[3] Compare 1 Corinthians, ii. 14.

[4] Alluding to the *Hadis*, "Reject not questioners."

QUESTION I.

First of all I am perplexed about my own thought;
What is that which they call thinking?

ANSWER I.[1]

You say, "Tell me what is 'thinking,'
"Since I am perplexed as to its meaning."
Thinking is passing from the false to the truth,
And seeing the Absolute Whole in the part.
Philosophers who have written books on it,
Say as follows when they are defining it,
That when a conception[2] is formed in the mind,
It is first of all named reminiscence.[3]
And when you pass on from this in thinking,[4]
It is called by the learned interpretation.[5]
When conceptions are properly arranged in the mind,
The result with logicians is known as thinking.
From proper arrangement of known conceptions
The unknown proposition[6] becomes known.
The major premiss is a father, the minor a mother,
And the conclusion a son, O brother!

[1] Thinking is the means to reach knowledge of God, *m'arifat;* and thinking is of two kinds, logical demonstration, and spiritual illumination. L.

[2] *Tasawwur*, conception, "idea."

[3] *Tazakkar*, reminiscence, the *anamnesis* of Plato. All major premisses, or first principles, says Lahiji, are gained by intuition, or reminiscence of ideas known to the mind in a former state.

[4] Compare *Risala Shamsiya* 5, 'Part is intuitive and part is inferential and the result of thought, *i.e.* of such an arrangement of known things, that it leads to the knowledge of unknown things.' See Aristotle, *An Pri.* I. i. 6.

[5] *'Ibrat*, from *'abr*, passing over, interpretation, explication, probably a translation of Aristotle's *Peri Hermeneias*, which treats of propositions.

[6] *Tasdik*, assertion, verification, proposition, as in *Risala Shamsiya* 3.

80 But to learn of what kind this arrangement is,
Reference must be made to books of logic.
Moreover, unless divine guidance aids it,
Verily logic is mere bondage of forms.[1]
That road is long and hard, leave it,
Like Moses for a season cast away that staff.[2]
Come for a season into the "Valley of Peace,"[3]
Hear with faith the call, "*Verily I am God.*"
He that knows "The Truth,"[4] and to whom Unity is revealed,
Sees at the first glance the light of very Being.
85 Nay more, as he sees by illumination that pure Light,
He sees God first in everything that he sees;
Abstraction[5] is a condition of good thinking,
For then the lightning of divine guidance illumines us.
To him, whom God guides not into the road,
It will not be disclosed by use of logic.
Forasmuch as the philosopher is bewildered,
He sees in things nothing but the contingent;

[1] *Taklid.* See note on couplet 109.

[2] Koran, *Sura* XX. 14 and 11: "What is that in thy right hand, O Moses? He answered, It is my staff whereon I lean, and wherewith I beat down leaves for my flock. God said, Cast it down, O Moses! And he cast it down, and behold it became a serpent, which ran about .... And when he was come near unto it (the burning bush), a voice called to him, saying, O Moses, verily I am thy Lord, wherefore put off thy shoes, for thou art in the sacred Valley 'Towa.'"

[3] *I.e.*, the *tarikat*, or Sufi's progress and course of illumination which leads him to the true knowledge of God. L.

[4] The Truth, *Hakk*, is the usual Sufi expression for the Absolute Divine Being.

[5] *Tajrid*, stripping off, making bare, seclusion from the world, logical abstraction, purification from self. Lahiji explains it as 'Passing by the stages of carnal lusts, and mental operations, and human pleasures and relations, and emerging from the limitation of self, which veils man's real essence.' Similarly, Plotinus directs the mystical aspirant to 'simplify his nature,' that he may become identified with the infinite. And Dionysius, the pseudo-Areopagite, exhorts his disciple 'to abandon the senses and all operations of the intellect, all objects of sense and all objects of thought, and *ignorantly* to strive upwards towards union with Him who is above all essence and knowledge; inasmuch as by separation of himself from all things, he will be exalted to the super-essential radiance of the Divine darkness.'—Vaughan, Hours with the Mystics, I. 288.

From the contingent he seeks to prove the necessary,
Therefore is he bewildered at the essence of the necessary.
Sometimes he travels backwards in a circle,[1]
Sometimes he is imprisoned in the chain of proofs.
While his reason goes deep into phenomenal existence,
His feet are caught in the chain of proofs.
All things are manifested through their likes,
But "The Truth" has neither rival nor like,
Since "The Truth" has neither rival nor peer,
I know not how you can know Him.[2]
Necessary matter has no sample in contingent:[3]
How can man know it, tell me how?[4]
Fool that he is! for he seeks the blazing sun
By the dim light of a torch in the desert.

ILLUSTRATION.[5]

If the sun tarried always in one position,
And if his shining were all after one manner,

[1] He argues in a circle; proves one contingent proposition by another contingent, which in its turn is proved by the first, and so on in an endless circle. L.

[2] Sense supplies us with finite objects only, and reason has only these finite objects to work on. It cannot transcend them, or mount from them to the infinite.

[3] The figment of contingent being occurs for the first time in the fifth book of Plato's Republic. Being, he argues, is the object of knowledge, and not being of ignorance, and therefore opinion which lies between them must have an object of its own as well, and this object is intermediate or contingent being, which is and is not, and partakes both of existence and non-existence. On this Professor Jowett notes:—"Plato did not remark that the degrees of knowledge in the subject have nothing corresponding to them in the object. With him a word must answer to an idea, he could not conceive of an opinion which was an opinion about nothing."—Jowett's Plato, II. 59.

[4] Compare Hafiz, Ode 355 (Brockhaus' edition):

'But how can our eyes behold Thee as Thou art?
'As our sight is, so see we, and only in part.'

[5] *Tamsil*, simile, analogy in logic. Schmölders (Documenta Philosophiæ Arabum). This illustration was probably suggested by Ghazzali. See Lewes, History of Philosophy, II. 51.

None would know that these beams are from him,
There would be no distinction between kernel and husk.
Know the whole world is a beam of the light of "The Truth,"
Yet "The Truth" within it is concealed from manifestation;[1]
And since the light of "The Truth" alters not nor varies,
And is void of change and transitoriness,
So you fancy that this world of itself is permanent
And enduring always of its own nature.
A man who relies on far-sighted reason[2]
Has much bewilderment before him,
From far-sightedness of overweening reason
One derives philosophy, another the Incarnation.[3]
Reason cannot endure the light of that face,
Go! that you may behold it, seek another eye.
Since the two eyes of the philosopher see double,[4]
He is impotent to behold the unity of "The Truth."
From blindness arose the doctrine of 'Assimilation,'[5]
From one-eyedness that of God's remoteness.[6]
From the same cause arose false and vain Metempsychosis,[7]

[1] Compare Tennyson, 'The Higher Pantheism':
'The sun, the moon, the stars, the seas, the hills and the plains,
Are not these, O Soul, the vision of Him who reigns?
Is not the vision He, tho' He be not that which He seems?'

[2] Far-sighted reason goes astray because it looks afar off for "The Truth," which is nearer to us than our neck vein.' L.

[3] The philosopher regards necessary and contingent matter as two distinct entities, whereas there is only the 'One.' L.

[4] *Halul*, descending, descent of the Spirit, the incarnation of God in Christ. L. The Sufi sect called *Nasriah*, or *Haluliah*, held that God had descended into individual men. See Sale's Koran, Prelim. Discourse, 125; Malcolm's Persia, II. 271.

[5] *Tashbih*, assimilation. The "Assimilators," says Lahiji, liken God to a material body dwelling above the highest heaven, *'arsh*, (*i.e.* they are, as we should say, anthropomorphists). Lahiji says these two doctrines are erroneous apart, but true together. God is remote from contingency, but is connected with the phenomenal world in that it is His reflection.

[6] *Tanzih*, declaring God to be without an equal, exalted above, and remote from matter.

[7] *Tanasukh*, transmigration of souls.

Since it had its origin from defective sight.
He is like one born blind, cut off from perfection,
The man who follows the road of schism,[1]
Men of externals have ophthalmia in both eyes,[2]
For they see in external objects naught but the external.
The theologian[3] who has no perception of Unitarianism[4]
Is in utter darkness in clouds and bondage of dogmas;[5]
Whatever each says about Unity, more or less,
Affords a specimen of his own power of insight.
The Divine Essence is freed from where, how, and why.[6]
Let His glory be exalted above what men say of Him.[7]

[1] The schismatics, or Mutazzalites, deny the eternity, *baka*, of God, and are therefore debarred from attaining to true insight into the verities of things. L.

[2] The men of externals (*ahl i Zahir*) are dominated by externals, and do not penetrate to "The Truth" within them. L.

[3] The *Mutakallamin*, or scholastic theologians, are 'they who tread the road to Divine knowledge with the foot of logic and not of illumination.' L. *Al-kalam* is defined in the *Dabistan* as the science enabling one to confirm the truth of religion by logical demonstration, and thus corresponds to the scholasticism of mediæval Europe.

[4] *Tauhid*, Unification, Unitarianism, belief in God's unity, acknowledging that all things are One. See Answer VII. and Hafiz (Brockhaus' edition), Ode 465:

'Hafiz, when preaching unity, with Unitarian pen
Blot out and cancel every page that tells of spirits and men.'

In the *Dabistan*, chapter xi., is given a list of the principal technical terms of the Muhammadan faith, with their exoteric or ordinary meanings, and with the esoteric meanings given to them by Miyan Bayazid, a Punjabi Sufi. The work of *Tauhid* is said to be "To annihilate self in the absolute Truth, and to become eternal in the Absolute, and to be made one with the One, and to abstain from evil."

[5] *Taklid*, putting a collar on the neck, blind imitation, canting, bondage, subservience to authority; compare the definition of *religio* from *religare*. Old women's religion is said to consist of *taklid*. The perfected Sufi advances from the stage of bondage, *taklid*, to that of absolute liberty and consciousness of truth, *itlak wa tahkik*. Compare St. Paul's expressions, "carnal ordinances," "law of a carnal commandment," "the yoke of bondage."

[6] *I.e.*, from quantity, quality, and relation. He is therefore incognoscible by the mind of man so long as it is not 'illumined' by Divine grace. L.

[7] Koran, *Sura* XVI. 3: 'Let Him be exalted above the gods they join with Him.'

QUESTION II.

What sort of thought is the condition of my path?
Wherefore is it sometimes a duty, sometimes a sin?

ANSWER II.

To think on the mercies is the condition of your path,[1]
But to think on the essence of "The Truth" is grievous sin.
Thinking on the essence of "The Truth" is vain;
Know it is impossible to demonstrate the manifest.[2]
Since His works are manifested from His essence,
His essence is not manifested from His works.[3]
The whole universe is exposed to view by His light,—
But how is He exposed to view in the universe?[4]
The light of His essence is not contained in phenomena,
For the glory of His majesty is exceeding great.
Let reason go, and abide in "The Truth."
The eye of a bat endures not the bright sun.
In that place where God's light is our guide,
What room is there for the message of Gabriel?[5]
Though the angels stand hard by the throne,
They reach not the station, '*I am with God.*'[6]

[1] Alluding to the *Hadis*, 'Think on the mercies of God, not on the essence of God.'

[2] *Tahsil i hasil*, "The Truth" is more general than His works, and thus demonstrating Him from His works is demonstrating the general and more known from the particular and less known. And again, knowledge of God is gained by illumination and intuition, and demonstration of ultimate facts of consciousness is impossible. L.

[3] *Aiat*, texts, names of God, works or signs of God.

[4] The face of "The Truth" is not displayed till all the illusory phenomena, which veil it, are annihilated. L. 'But is it unreasonable to confess that we believe in God not by reason of the nature which conceals him, but by reason of the supernatural in man which reveals him?'—Jacobi, quoted in Hamilton's Metaphysics, I. 40.

[5] Gabriel was the "angel of revelation." See Koran, *Sura* II. 91.

[6] This refers to the tradition, 'There are times when I am with God in such wise that neither highest angel nor prophet apostle can attain thereto.'

Like as His light utterly burns up the angels,[1]
So it burns up reason from head to foot.
Reason's light applied to the very Light of lights,
Is as the eye of the head applied to the sun.
When the object seen is very near to the eye,
The eye is darkened so that it cannot see it.[2]
This blackness,[3] if you know it, is the light of very Being;
In the land of darkness is the well-spring of life.[4]
Since the dark destroys the light of vision,
Give up looking, for this is no place for looking.[5]
What connection has the dust with the pure world?
Its perception is impotence to perceive perception.[6]
Blackness of face[7] is not divorced from the contingent
In the two worlds; *Allah is all wise.*

[1] All phenomena are annihilated in Him. L.

[2] The mental bewilderment or darkness which occurs to the mystic is the light of Absolute Being approaching close to him. L.

[3] See a passage of Dionysius, the pseudo-Arcopagite, quoted in Tholuck (Blüthensammlung aus der Morgenländischen Mystik), p. 9: "Then is he delivered from all things seeing or being seen, and dives down into the truly mystical darkness of ignorance, wherein he closes up all the intellectual apprehensions, and finds himself in the utterly impalpable and invisible, being entirely in Him who is beyond all, and in none else, either himself or another; being united as to his nobler part with the utterly unknown by the cessation of all knowing, and at the same time, in that very knowing nothing, knowing what transcends the mind of man." And Blosius (quoted in Vaughan, I. 290): "The light is called dark from its excessive brightness."

[4] Alluding to the "water of life" found by the prophet Khizr in the land of darkness.

[5] When the mystic annihilates all phenomena, self included, which veil the face of "The Truth," and is drawn near to, and united with "The Truth," seer and seen are identified, and looking is no longer possible.

[6] The dust, *i.e.* the contingent is naught but the reflection in not being of Necessary Being, which in itself is pure from the stain of contingency and plurality. Therefore the contingent is impotent to perceive "The Truth" in the ordinary way, and its highest degree of perception is to be absorbed in the "The Truth," when its eyes are blinded by excess of light, and its vision is unconsciousness,—inability to be conscious of seeing. L.

[7] Blackness of face=nothingness, not being. The contingent is naught but not being, and its highest perfection is to be conscious of this, and to annihilate self by absorption in "The Truth." L.

Blackness of face in both worlds is poverty,[1]
Blackness is most precious, neither more nor less.
What shall I say? since this saying is fine,
'A light night that shineth in a dark day.'[2]
On this place of witnessing which is the light of Epiphany,[3]
I have much to say, but not to say it is best.

Illustration.

If you desire to behold the eye of the sun,
You must make use of another body;
Since the eye of the head has not strength enough,
You may look on the brilliant sun in the water.
Since its brightness shows less brightly therein,
You can bear to look on it for a longer space.
Not being[4] is the mirror of absolute Being,
Therein is reflected the shining of "The Truth."
When Not being is set opposite to Being,
It catches its reflection in a moment.
That Unity is exposed to view in this plurality,
Like as when you count one it becomes many.

[1] Referring to the *Hadis*, 'Poverty is my peace.' Poverty with the Sufis means self annihilation.

[2] This darkness is light, because it shows "The Truth," free from the veil of plurality. It shines in a day, *i. e.* the visible world of phenomena, but this day is dark because phenomena veil "The Truth." L.

[3] Divine Epiphanies, such as that to Moses at the burning bush, and to Mohammad on the night of his ascension. See couplet 367.

[4] *'Adm*, privation of being, not being. The '*to me on*' of the Eleatics, handed on to the Sufis through Plato, Plotinus and the Arabian philosophers. See Jami, *Tuhfat-ul-Inrar*. *Mokamat*, I.:—

'In its cradle lay with suspended breath
The infant of creation in the sleep of not being.
The eyes of that Beauty seeing what was not
Beheld the non-existent as existent.
Though he beheld in His own perfections
The beauties of all things and their qualities,
Yet He desired that in another mirror
They might be displayed to His view.'

Though all numbers have one for their starting point,
Nevertheless you never come to the end of them.
Forasmuch as Not being in itself is pure,
Therein is reflected '*The hidden treasure.*'
Read the tradition '*I was a hidden treasure,*'[1]
That you may see clearly this concealed mystery.
Not being is the mirror, the world the reflection, and man
Is as the reflected eye of The unseen Person.
You are that reflected eye, and He the light of the eye,
In that eye His eye sees His own eye.[2]
The world is a man and man is a world:[3]
There is no clearer explanation than this.
When you look well into the root of this matter,
He is at once seer, seeing eye, and thing seen.
The holy tradition[4] has declared this,
And, '*without eye or ear,*' demonstrated it.
Know the world is a mirror from head to foot,[5]
In every atom are a hundred blazing suns.
If you cleave the heart of one drop of water,
A hundred pure oceans emerge from it.
If you examine closely each grain of dust,
A thousand Adams may be seen in it.

[1] Alluding to the tradition, 'David inquired, saying, O Lord, why hast Thou created mankind? God said, I was a hidden treasure, and I desired to become known, and I created the world in order to be known.'

[2] Compare a somewhat similar passage in the *Khândogya Upanishad*, VIII., 7—12, quoted in Max Müller's Hibbert Lectures, 318—321. 'Man,' says Lahiji, 'is the eye of the world, whereby God sees his own works.' Compare Hegel. M. Müller, Hibbert Lectures, 20.

[3] Man, being the epitome of all the Divine names and qualities, is the microcosm, and the world is 'the great man,' because it bears to man, 'the eye of the world,' the relation of a man to one of his members. L. Compare George Herbert:—

'Man is one world, and hath another to attend him.'

[4] "My servant draws nigh to me by pious works till I love him, and when I love him, I am his eye, his ear, his tongue, his foot, his hand, and by me he sees, hears, alks, walks, and tastes." L.

[5] Through this process of reflection every atom is potentially a mirror of any and all the Divine names and qualities, and when any atom puts off its limitation and phenomenal character it becomes "the All." L.

In its members a gnat is like an elephant,
In its qualities a drop of rain is like the Nile.
The heart of a barley-corn equals a hundred harvests,
A world dwells in the heart of a millet seed.
In the wing of a gnat is the ocean of life,[1]
In the pupil of the eye a heaven.
What though the corn grain of the heart[2] be small,
It is a station for the Lord of both worlds to dwell therein.
Therein are gathered the two worlds,
Sometimes Iblis and sometimes Adam.[3]
Behold the world mingled together,
Angels with demons, Satan with the archangel.
All mingled like unto seed and fruit,
Infidel with faithful, and faithful with infidel.
Together are gathered, in the point of the present,[4]
All cycles and seasons, day, month, and year.
World without beginning is world without end,
The mission of Jesus falls with the creation of Adam.[5]
From every point in this concatenated circle
A thousand forms are drawn;
Every point as it revolves in a circle
Is now a centre, now a circling circumference.[6]

[1] *I.e.*, absolute Being. L.

[2] The heart's core,—the drop of black blood in the heart, supposed by Muhammadans to be the principle of life. L.

[3] Adam is a manifestation of the Divine beauty, *jamal,* and Iblis of Divine majesty and wrath, *jalal.* L.

[4] Compare:

'Nothing is there to come, and nothing past,
But an eternal *now* does always last.'
Cowley, Davideis, I. 302.

[5] The last event in Divine history coincides in point of time with the first. All things, whatever the times of their manifestations, are present together in God. There is no time in God. L.

[6] There is one great circle of emanations down to man, and back to God, and smaller circles caused by each particular emanation having a course of its own, *e.g.*, universal reason revolves in all particular reasons. Each link is potentially all, and hence destruction of one is destruction of all. L.

If you take one atom link from its place
The entire universe falls to ruin.
The whole in a dizzy whirl, and yet no single part
Placing foot beyond the limit of contingency,
Phenomenal being[1] holding each one in bondage,
Each is in despair at its particularization from the Whole.
You may say each is ever travelling and yet restrained,
Each is ever being unclothed and clothed upon;[2]
Each is alway in motion, yet ever at rest,
Never beginning and never ending.
Each ever cognizant of his own essence, and for that cause
Ever pressing his way towards the throne on high.
Beneath the veil of each atom is hidden
The heart-ravishing beauty of the Beloved's face!

Rule I.[3]

You have heard thus much of the universe,
Come, say what you have seen of the universe.
What know you of form or of substance?
What is the next world, and what is this world?
Say what is Simurg, and what mount Kaf,[4]
What heaven and hell, and hades[5] what?

[1] *Ta'ayyun*, phenomenalization or emanation, evidentiation. See note on couplet 273 and couplet 484.

[2] This is an allusion to Koran, *Sura* L. 14: "Yet are they in doubt (or being clothed with, *labas*), a new creation." Each atom non-existent in itself is being every moment clothed with a fresh phenomenal efflux from Absolute Being, and again stripped of it. When it strips off the phenomenal it is united with the Absolute, and when it again puts it on, it is held back from union and "travaileth in bondage." L.

[3] These rules are an elaboration of the thesis that knowledge of the Truth is to be attained not by sense and reason but by illumination. L.

[4] Simurg, a fabulous bird, said to dwell on Mount Kaf, or Caucasus,—the type of Supreme Being and plurality in Unity.

[5] *Al'araf* or *Barzakh*, the partition, veil, or "barrier" between death and the resurrection, or between this world and the next, a hades or purgatory, in which the dead are examined by Munkir and Nakir.—Sale, Koran, Prelim. Disc. 55, and *Sura* XXIII. 102.

What is that world which is not seen,
One day whereof equals a year of this world?
That world, in fine, is not what you see.
Have you not heard the text, '*What ye see not?*'[1]
Come, show me what is Jabulca,[2]
What that city whose name is Jabulsa.
Consider the East along with the West,
For this world contains no more than one of each.[3]
Come and hear the meaning of '*like unto them*;'[4]
Hear it from Ibn Abbas, and then know yourself!
You are asleep, and this vision of yours is a dream,
All that you see thereby is an illusion.
On the morn of the last day, when you shall awake,
You will know all this to be the baseless fabric of fancy.
When the illusion of seeing double is removed,
Earth and heavens will become transfigured.
When the true Sun displays his face to you[5]
There remains not the light of Venus, moon or sun.
Falls one beam of His on the hard rock,
It is torn to pieces like wool of divers colours.[6]
Know now is the time that you have power to act:
What profit is there in knowing, when you are powerless?[7]

[1] Koran, *Sura* LXIX. 38.

[2] Sale, Prelim. Disc. 83, explains these as the celestial and terrestrial Jerusalem, Lahiji as the worlds of ideals, and of disembodied spirits. He says one of them lies in the east, the other in the west. See Gal. iv. 26, and Deutsch, Islam. p. 101.

[3] Sense tells us nothing of the unseen worlds. L.

[4] See Slane's Ibn Khallikan, i. 89, note. The saying referred to is, "If I explained to you the verse, 'God created seven heavens and earths like unto them' ye would stone me, or call me unbeliever." See Koran, *Sura* LXV. 12.

[5] The Father of lights.—James i. 17.

[6] 'On that day the mountains shall become like carded wool of divers colours.'—Koran, *Sura* CI. 4.

[7] Man by reason of the universality of his nature, *i.e.* his comprehending in him self all the divers names and attributes of "The Truth," is capable of apprehending Divine Epiphanies, and attaining to knowledge of "The Truth," and should set himself to do this while his powers are in their prime. L.

How shall I tell the tale of 'states' of heart[1]
To you, O man, with head downcast and feet in the mire?
The world is yours and yet you remain indigent.
Has man ever seen one so pitiable as you are?
Like captives you are confined to one spot,
Binding your feet with your own helpless hand.
You sit like women in the street of ill fortune,
You take no shame to yourself for your ignorance.
The valiant of the world are rolling in carnage;
You, with head wrapped up, put not forth your foot.
How read you the text, "*old woman's creed,*"
That you hold ignorance to be lawful for you?
Whereas "women are wanting in intellect and faith,"[2]
Why should men choose their road?
If you are a man, come forth and pass on,
Whatever hinders you, pass aside by it.
Tarry not day or night at the halting places,[3]
Linger not behind your fellow travellers and camels.
Like 'The Friend of God,' go seek "The Truth,"[4]
Turn night into day and day into night.[5]
Stars with moon and most brilliant sun
Represent sense, imagination and brilliant reason.[6]
Turn your face from all these, O pilgrim,
Say alway, '*I love not them that set.*'

[1] *I.e.* ecstatic states in which Divine Epiphanies and visions are displayed to the eart. L.

[2] There is another tradition, "an old woman's creed is yours." Lahiji says it is nere bondage, *taklid*, mechanical religion, cant. Compare 1 Tim. iv. 7, 'old vives' fables.'

[3] Compare Hafiz, Ode I.

[4] "And when the night overshadowed him, Abraham saw a star and he said, 'This s my Lord;' but when it set, he said, 'I like not gods which set.' And when he aw the moon rising, he said, 'This is my Lord;' but when he saw it set, he said, Verily, if my Lord direct me not, I shall become one of them that go astray.'"— Koran, *Sura* VI. 77.

[5] Relax not your efforts at any season. L.

[6] *Hiss i mushtarak*, the *koine aisthesis* of Aristotle.

Like Moses, son of Amran, press onwards in this road,
Till you hear the words, '*Verily I am God.*'[1]
So long as the mount of your being remains[2] before you,
The answer to '*Show me*' is '*Thou shalt not see me.*'[3]
"The Truth," as amber, attracts you like a straw.
If there were no mount of "youness," where were the road?[4]
When its Lord appears in glory to the mount of existence,
Existence is laid low, even as the dust of the road.
The beggar becomes by one attraction a king,
In one instant it makes the mount as a straw.[5]
Follow the steps of the prophet in his ascension,
Marvel at all the mighty signs.[6]
Come forth from the dwelling of Umhâni,[7]
Say only, "*Whoso hath seen me hath seen The Truth.*"[8]
Forsake the *Kaf* of the corner of both worlds,
Sit on mount *Kaf* at "*the distance of two bows' lengths.*"[9]

[1] Alluding to the burning bush (Koran, *Sura* XXVIII. 31), *i.e.* till you are illumined by Divine Epiphanies.

[2] The mount, *i.e.* phenomenal illusive existence, which hides real absolute Being. L.

[3] Alluding to the giving of the law on Mount Sinai. "And when Moses came at the appointed time, and his Lord spake unto him, he said, 'O Lord, show me thy self, that I may behold thee.' God answered, 'Thou shalt in no wise behold me, but look towards the mountain, and if it stand firm in its place, then thou shalt see me.' But when his Lord appeared with glory in the mount He reduced it to dust, and Moses fell on his face in a swoon and was beside himself."—Koran, *Sura* VII. 139.

[4] Amber is called *kah raba*, attractor of straws. When your phenomenal existence, your 'youness,' is swept away, there is no longer any interval between you and God. L. There is here a play on the word "*tui*," which means "firm" as well as "youness."

[5] The attraction of Divine graces enriches the fakir or beggar (*i.e.* the man who is 'poor in spirit' and stripped of self), with the wealth of union with the Absolute. L.

[6] *I.e.* Divine Epiphanies. L.

[7] The daughter of Abu Talib, from whose house the prophet started on his ascension to heaven.

[8] This saying is ascribed to Muhammad in the *Maksad-i-Aksa.*—Palmer, 97. Cf. John xiv. 9.

[9] "Afterwards he (Muhammad) approached near until he was at the distance of

"The Truth" will then grant you whatsoever you ask,
And show you all things *as they really are.*[1]

Rule II.

To him, whose soul attains the beatific vision,[2]
The universe is the book of "The Truth Most High."
Accidents are its vowels, and substance its consonants,
And grades of creatures its verses and pauses.
Therein every world is a special chapter,
One the chapter *Fatihah*, another *Ikhlas*.
Of this book the first verse is 'Universal Reason,'[3]
For that is like the *B* of *Bismillah*;
Second comes "Universal Soul," 'the verse of light,'[4]
For that is as a lamp of exceeding light;
The third verse thereof is "Highest heaven."[5]

two bows' length from Him in heaven."—Koran, *Sura* LIII. 9. Mount Kaf was the abode of the Simurg, the type of Absolute Being.

[1] Alluding to the *Hadis*, 'Inspiration is a light that descends into the heart and shows the nature of things as they really are.' The illumined Sufi sees 'things as they are' when after annihilation of self, *fana*, he endures and abides (*baka*) in God. L.

[2] The author here describes the successive "emanations" of Divinity under the figure of the successive chapters of the Koran. The Alexandrian doctrine of "emanations"—intermediate potencies or intelligences by whom God acts on the world of phenomena—"links between the Divine spirit and the world of matter,"—seems to have sprung from an amalgamation of the ancient Persian angelology—the *Amshaspands*, *Izads*, and *Fravâshis*,—with Greek Ontology, the "ideas" of Plato, the *logos* of Philo, the *nous* of Plotinus. (See Deutsch. Remains, p. 50, and Mansel, Gnostic Heresies, p. 26). This doctrine pervades the entire Neoplatonist philosophy, and the writings of the Gnostics, (see Ueberweg, Greek Philosophy, I. 224), and re-appears in the systems of the Muhammadan philosophers Al Farabi, 950 A.D., Avenpace, circ. 1118 A.D., and Averroes, circ. 1150 A.D. (Ueberweg, I. pp. 412—417), and in the Jewish Kabbala.

[3] Universal Reason (*'akl-i-kull*) and Universal Soul (*nufs* or *jan-i-kull*) are translations of the Neoplatonic *logos* and *pneuma*. See *'Aiun-ul-masâil* by Abu Nasr Al Farabi, and the remarks of Schmölders (Documenta Philosophiæ Arabum, p. 96). The *'Aiun-ul-masâil* is a summary of Aristotelian metaphysics as interpreted by the Alexandrian Neoplatonist commentators.

[4] Koran, *Sura* XXIV. 36, 'a light from the oil of a blessed tree.'

[5] Koran, *Sura* VII. 55, *'arsh*, or heaven of heavens.

Read the fourth verse, it is "The throne;"[1]
After that are the seven heavenly spheres,
The "chapter of the seven limbs" answers to these.[2]
After these, behold the bodies of the four elements,
Whereof each answers to its respective verse.
After these come the three kingdoms of nature,
Whose verses you cannot count.
The last that came down was the soul of man,[3]
And thus the Koran ends with the chapter "Men."

Rule III.

THOUGHTS ON THE HEAVENS.

Rest not in bondage in the prison of nature,
Come forth and behold the divine handiwork.
Consider the structure of the heavens,
So that you may praise "The Truth" for His signs.[4]
Look up and see how the vault of "highest heaven"[5]
Is stretched round about both worlds.
Wherefore do they name it "throne of the Merciful?"
What connection has it with the heart of man?[6]
Wherefore are these two continually in motion,
Never for a moment taking rest?
Peradventure the heart is the centre of that heaven,
Heart the central point and heaven the circumference.[7]

[1] Koran, *Sura* II. 256, the eighth heaven.

[2] *Sura* I., which contains seven divisions, or the seven chapters from *Bakrat* to *Taubat*. Seven heavens are mentioned in the Talmud, and the 'third heaven' is mentioned in 2 Corinthians xii. 2. Compare *Sura* II. 27: "Into seven heavens did He fashion it."

[3] *Nazil*, 'coming down,' is the term for the revelation of a verse in the Koran.

[4] Or, 'in verses of the Koran.' L.

[5] *I. e.*, *'arsh*, the ninth heaven.

[6] Alluding to the *Hadis*: "The heart of the believer is the highest heaven." The *'arsh* and the heart of man are both theatres of Divine perfections, and the *'arsh*, as the less perfect, may be subsidiary to the heart, the more perfect theatre. L. See couplet 652.

[7] See couplet 796.

In the space of one day and night, more or less,
Highest heaven surpasses your circuits, O Durvesh![1]
Moved by this the other heavenly spheres are circling:
Mark well how they all move in one direction.
From east to west, like a water-wheel,
They are ever hastening, without food or sleep.
Each day and night this highest sphere
Makes a complete revolution round the world.
Moved by this, the other heavenly spheres
Are revolving in circular orbits in like manner,
But contrary to the rotation of the crystalline sphere,[2]
These eight lower spheres revolve crookedly.[3]
The Ecliptic holds the signs of the zodiac,[4]
In them is no interval nor any interstice.
Aries and Taurus, and Gemini and Cancer,
Are hung upon it with Leo and Virgo.[5]
Then Libra and Scorpio, then Sagittarius,
Capricorn, and Aquarius, and then the sign Pisces,
The fixed stars are one thousand twenty and four,
Who have their stations round about the "throne."[6]

[1] Alluding to the *taw'af*, or perambulations of shrines made by Durweshes. L.

[2] According to the Ptolemaic scheme the seven planets with their respective spheres, "cycle and epicycle, orb on orb," constitute the solar system. Beyond this is the eighth sphere, that of the fixed stars, and beyond that the crystalline, or ninth sphere, to which was attributed a certain 'trepidation' to account for the irregularities observed in the motion of the fixed stars. Beyond this was the *primum mobile*, the sphere which was at once first moved and the first mover, communicating its motion to the lower spheres revolving within it. Beyond the *primum mobile* was the empyrean. Ptolemy's *Syntaxis Magna* was translated into Arabic by Ishak bin Hossain, under the title *Al Megiste*, about 800 A.D. Apparently Lahiji takes the crystalline sphere, *charkh i atlas*, to be the same as the *charkh i 'azam*, or highest sphere.

[3] Literally, 'bent as a bow.' The eighth sphere and those beneath it move with two motions, one east to west like the highest sphere, and secondly west to east. L.

[4] The Ecliptic is also called the 'girdle' of the 'throne,' or eighth sphere. L.

[5] Virgo, *Khushah*, which also means a bunch of grapes, and is therefore said to be hung up. L.

[6] The eighth heaven.

Of the seventh heaven Saturn is the watchman,
The sixth is the mansion and house of Jupiter,
The fifth heaven is the house of Mars,
The fourth of the Sun, adorner of the earth,
The third of Venus, the second of Mercury:
The Moon holds its orbit on the sphere of the Earth.
The house of Saturn is in Capricorn and Aquarius,
Jupiter waxes and wanes in Sagittarius and Pisces.[1]
In Aries and Scorpio is found the place of Mars,
In Leo is the Sun's place of rest;
Like as Venus makes her house in Taurus and Libra,
So does Mercury abide in Gemini and Virgo.
The Moon sees in Cancer a creature akin to herself,
When head becomes tail she assumes the form of a knot.[2]
The Moon passes through eight and twenty mansions,[3]
And then she returns opposite to the Sun.[4]
Then she becomes like to a *crooked palm-branch*,[5]
By command of the Almighty who is Allwise.
If you think on this, as a perfect man,
Assuredly you will say, 'All this is not vain.'[6]
The words of "The Truth" are clear on this point,[7]
That to call this vain is weakness of faith.

[1] The "houses" of the planets are those signs of the zodiac in which they attain their maximum ascension. L.

[2] The points where the moon's orbit cuts the ecliptic are called 'knots,' and the portions of her orbit north and south of the ecliptic are called respectively the "head" and "tail of the dragon." L.

[3] "And for the moon have we appointed certain mansions, until she change and return to be like the old branch of a palm tree."—Koran, *Sura* XXXVI. 28. These *anwa*, or mansions, are the divisions of the zodiac, through one of which the moon passes each night.

[4] *I. e.* becomes full. L.

[5] *I. e.* in her last quarter. L.

[6] "The course of nature is the art of God."—Young, Night Thoughts, IX. 1267.

[7] *Batil*, 'Vain, what is without God.'—*Istilahat us Sufiat*, p. 14. Koran, *Sura* III. 138: "Think on the creation of the heavens and the earth. Have we created them in vain?"

O fool, the body of a gnat enshrines wisdom,[1]
Then how is there no wisdom in Mercury and Mars?
Albeit if you look into the roots of this matter,
You see the heavens subject to the Almighty.[2]
When the astrologer is destitute of religion, and says
That starry influences proceed from the heavenly motions,[3]
He sees not that these revolving heavens
Are all under the sway and dominion of "The Truth."

Illustration.

You may say these heavens are revolving
In the rotation of day and night like a potter's wheel.
And thereby every moment the wisdom of the Master
Fashions a new vessel out of water and clay.
Whatever exists in time and in space
Proceeds from one master hand, one workshop.
The stars, who are of the people of perfection,[4]
Wherefore are they always undergoing the defect of setting?
Why are they continually varying in position,
In place and orbit, in colour and size?
Why are they now in Nadir, now in Zenith?
Sometimes in opposition, sometimes in conjunction?
Wherefore again is the heart of heaven fretted with fire?
What does it desire that it is always in a whirl?
All the planets circling round in search of this,
Sometimes above, sometimes beneath the earth?
The elements water, air, fire and earth
Have taken their station below the heavens;

[1] See Koran, *Sura* II. 24.

[2] On the one hand it is wrong to deny the wisdom manifested in the structure of the heavens, and on the other hand it is equally wrong to say with the astrologer that they are self moved, and govern things on earth. L.

[3] Compare "The sweet influences of the Pleiades." Job xxxviii. 31.

[4] This idea is found in Aristotle. *Nicom. Eth.* vi. 7. 4. The perfection of a star is its ascension, and its defect its setting. L.

Each serving diligently in its own appointed place,
Before or behind which it never sets its foot.
Though all four are contrary in their nature and position,
Still one may see them ever united together.[1]
Inimical are they to each other in essence and form
Yet united into single bodies by fiat of necessity.[2]
From them is born the three-fold kingdom of Nature,
Minerals, then plants, then animals,
Setting up substance in their midst,[3]
As Sufis becoming pure from form.[4]
All at the command and by favour of the Master,
Standing in their places subject to His will,
The minerals by His wrath laid low in the dust,
The plants by His favour standing erect,
The sexual passion of animals with ardour unfeigned
Preserving their genera, species, and individuals,
All confessing the rule of their Master,
Searching out His will day and night!

Rule IV.

THOUGHTS ON SOULS.

Ponder well once for all on your own origin,
Your first mother had a father who was also her mother.[5]
Behold the world entirely comprised in yourself,

[1] *I.e.*, in compound bodies. All these are proofs of the entire subjection of all things to one primal agent, "The Truth." L.

[2] Compare Burke: "From the reciprocal struggle of discordant powers is drawn out the harmony of the universe."

[3] *Haiuli*, substance, is the Greek *He Hyle*,—explained in *Istilahat us Sufiat*, p. 25, as the inward element in things as opposed to the outward form,—the *hypokeimenon*, 'that which underlies,' *quod substat*.

[4] When the simple elements are united into compounds, each element drops its own 'form,' and is blended with the others into one common substance. L.

[5] Universal Reason, the first emanation from the Absolute, is likened to Adam; and Universal Soul, the second emanation, to Eve, since Universal Soul was evolved out of Universal Reason, like Eve out of Adam's rib. L.

That which was made last was first in thought.[1]
The last that was made was the soul of Adam,
The two worlds were a means to his production.
There is no other final cause beyond man,
It is disclosed in man's own self.[2]
The black hearted and the fool are the opposites of light
Yet are they the theatres of the true epiphany.[3]
When the back of a mirror is blackened,
It will reflect a man's face from its face ;[4]
And the rays of the sun in the fourth heaven
Are not reflected till they fall on the dust of earth.
You are the reflection of "The Adored of angels,"
For this cause are you worshipped of angels.[5]
Each creature that goes before you has a soul,
And from that soul is bound a cord to you.[6]
Therefore are they all subject to your dominion,
For that the soul of each one is hidden in you,
You are the kernel of the world in the midst thereof,
Know yourself that you are the world's soul.

[1] Universal Reason is also the 'very essence of man,' so that what was first in the Divine thought, was the last in fact. Man was thus the final cause of creation. L.

[2] All things were created as subsidiary to man, but man is an end in himself, and not a means to any further end. L.

[3] This refers to Koran, *Sura* XXXIII. 72 : 'Verily, we proposed a deposit to the heavens, and to the earth, and to the mountains between them, but they refused the burden, and we entrusted it to man, who is unjust (or 'dark') and foolish.' This deposit is the duty of displaying the Divine attributes, and man does this through the universality of his nature, containing "the fullness of the Godhead." He is good on one side and evil on the other,—"created half to rise and half to fall." The good represents the beautiful attributes of God *(jamal)*, and the evil the terrible attributes *(jalal)*. L.

[4] Man, the mirror of Divinity, is on one side blackened with the darkness of Not Being, in order to reflect Very Being. L.

[5] "And He said unto the angels, 'Worship Adam,' and they all worshipped him except Iblis."—Koran, *Sura* II. 32.

[6] The 'essence of man,' or Universal Reason, is the soul which animates all things, and forms the bond of mystical union between them and man. L.

The north quarter of the world is your dwelling place,[1]
Because the heart is on the left side of the body.
The world of reason and mind is your stock in trade,
Earth and heavens are your vesture.
Behold this Not being which is the evidence[2] of Being,
See this height how it is the essence of depth.[3]
Your natural powers are ten thousand,[4]
Your volitions transcend limits and counting.
For that cause is each man[5] furnished with instruments,
With limbs, members, and sinews.
Physicians become bewildered at these,
And stand amazed at the anatomy of man.
Not one has mastered this science,
Who does not avow his ignorance thereof.
His limit and portion are appointed to each by "The Truth,"
Each arises from and returns to one Name.[6]
In that name each creature has its being,
To that name it is ever giving praise;
At its beginning each proceeds from that source,
At its return that is its door of departure.
By the door whereat each enters, it departs,
Though in its lifetime each wanders from door to door.[7]

[1] *Shamali*, north, also means left.

[2] *'Ayn*, eye, appearance, essence, reality. The "quality" of a proposition.—Schmölders (Documenta Philosophiæ Arabum), p. 130. *'Ayan i sabita*, the established evidences or epiphanies of the Divine "ideas," manifested in the phenomenal world; opposed to *'ayan i 'ilmiya*, the same "ideas" concealed in the 'intellectual presence' of God. 'Universal reason' is said to be in the Divine *'ilm* (knowledge), and man to be the same 'essence of man' manifested in *'ayn* (to outward view). Lahiji uses the expression, "the worlds of *'ilm* and *'ayn*." A name is called the *'ayn* of the thing named. See *Dabistan* (Calcutta edition), p. 456.

[3] 'Universal Reason,' the first emanation, is also the "essence of man," the lowest emanation. L.

[4] Natural, *i.e.* involuntary, such as digestion, growth, &c. L.

[5] Or "each power." L.

[6] Each creature or each power reflects some one of the Divine names or attributes. From this name each is first manifested and to this it returns. L.

[7] *Mubda*, beginning or origin, is said to be the stage of *wajud i 'ilmiat*; *ma'ash*,

Hence you learn all the names of God,
For that you are an image reflected from "The Named."[1]
Power and Knowledge and Will are shown forth
In you, O slave of the Lord of bliss!
You are the Hearing, Seeing, Living, Speaking,
Yet you endure not of yourself but of Him!
O first who are also the essence of the last!
O inner who are also the essence of the outward![2]
You day and night are cogitating about yourself,
It is most meet that you should think on self no more,[3]
Since the end of thought is bewilderment,[4]
This discourse on thought ends at this point.

QUESTION III.

What am I? tell me what "I" means?
What is the meaning of "Travel into yourself?"[5]

ANSWER III.

Again you question me, saying, "What am I?"
Give me news of myself as to what "I" means.
When Absolute Being has to be indicated

fetime or sustenance, that of *wajud i 'ayni*, *i.e.* the Divine ideas evolved to view. *'u'ad*, return, is the retrocession of the creature back to *wajud i 'ilmiat*. Each reature wanders about during its manifestation in forgetfulness of its origin. L.

[1] *I. e.*, God. The names which follow are those of the seven essential Divine ttributes. The argument is that since each creature is the manifestation of some ne Name of God, and you are the epitome of all creatures, therefore you see in yourlf reflections of all the names of God. L.

[2] Koran, *Sura* LVII. 3.

[3] By no process of logic or thought can you escape from egoism and tuism, and ttain to true knowledge, so it is better for you to renounce the attempt to reach nowledge by thought. L.

[4] When the thinker and the object of his thought become united, thinking is no nger possible, for thinking implies duality. The end of thought is (when union kes place) bewilderment,—dazzling of the mental eye, owing to its proximity to The Truth." L.

[5] Alluding to the *Hadis*—'Whoso knows himself knows his Lord.' *Introrsum ascen re* has been the watchword of mystics in all ages.

Men use the word "I" to express it.
When "The Truth" is set in evidence in a phenomenon
You express it by the word "I,"[1]
"I" and "you" are the accidents[2] of Very Being.
The lattices of the niches of the lamp of Necessary Being.[3]
Know bodies and spirits are all the One Light,
Now shining from mirrors, now from torches.
You say "The word 'I' in every connection"
"Indicates the reasonable soul of man;"
But as you have made human intellect your guide,
You do not know your 'self' from one of your parts,
Go, O master, and know well your 'self,'
For fatness does not resemble an empty tumour.[4]
"I" and "you" are higher than body and soul,
For both body and soul are parts of "me."
The word "I" is not limited to man,
So that you should say it means only the soul.[5]
  Straightway lift yourself above time and space,[6]
Quit the world and be yourself a world for yourself.[7]

[1] Absolute Being in regard of its remoteness from relations and attributes is no indicated in any phenomenon, but in regard of its accidental connexion with th visible universe it is indicated by the phenomenon 'man's self,' 'I' and 'you.' L.

[2] *'Ariz*, a logical accident.—*Risalah Shamsiyah* (translated by Sprenger), page 7 The one Light shines with many rays through the lattices of various personalities. L

[3] Alluding to Koran, *Sura* XXIV. 35: 'Allah is the light of the heavens and th earth, and the likeness of His light is as a lamp, wherein is a torch, and the torc in a glass, and the glass shining as a star with the oil of a blessed tree.' Bodie are likened to mirrors, and spirits to torches.

[4] Fatness, *i. e.* the real knowledge gained by illumination, is not like the empty puffed up conceit of intellect. L.

[5] 'I' and 'You' are the theatres of Absolute Being in its entirety, whereas body and soul are exponents of single Divine attributes only. L.

[6] This is a very favourite precept of mystical philosophers and theologians. See th passages from St. Augustine, Tauler, Swedenborg, Silesius, Schelling, and Schleier-macher, quoted in Mansel's Bampton Lectures, p. 250. It amounts to this, that t know the infinite man must himself be infinite (*ib.*, p. 58).

[7] Here begins the answer to the second clause of the question. It is to become annihilated (*fani*) in your 'self,' and enduring (*baki*) in God. L.

By the imaginary line of the H of the "He"[1]
Are produced two eyes at the time He looks forth.[2]
But there remain not in the midst pilgrim or road,
When this H of the "He" is joined to the H in Allah.
Necessary Being is as Heaven and Hell as contingent,
"I" and "you" are the Hades veil between them.[3]
When this veil is lifted up from before you,[4]
There remains not the bond of sects and creeds.
All the authority of the law is over this "I" of yours,
Since that is bound to your soul and body.[5]
When "I" and "you" remain not in the midst,
What is mosque, what is synagogue, what is fire temple?
Phenomenal being is as the dot on *'ayn*,
When *'ayn* is clear, *ghayn* becomes *'ayn*.[6]
The journey of the pilgrim is two steps and no more,
Although it is beset by divers perils.
One step is the passing out from that H of "He,"[7]

[1] *Huwiyat*, 'Ipseity.' (Sprenger, *Risalah Shamsiyah*, p. 7.) *Hu*, He=God; *Yahu*=Jehovah (Shea's *Dabistan*, III. 222, note).

[2] Alluding to the form of the round *H*. The "looking" is explained by the passage from Jami quoted in the note to couplet 134. The *H* of *Huwiyat* (Divine Ipseity) is the phenomenon manifesting absolute Being in the visible universe. Thus we have duality 'I' and 'He,' but this duality is only imaginary, and vanishes as soon as 'I' and 'He' are united by mystical union in Allah. Compare couplet 142. L.

[3] 'I' is the phenomenon displaying Absolute Being in its entirety,—its *jamal*, or beauty, as well as its *jalal*, or terror and evil. Hence it is as a veil or wall of partition between Heaven, the analogue of necessary and good being, and Hell contingent and evil being. L.

[4] The Sufis call whatever opposes perfect union with the Divinity a "veil." See a saying of Junaid quoted in his life in *Nafhat ul uns*, p. 92.

[5] It is only in consequence of man's phenomenal extrusion from Divinity, and his individual personality embracing evil as well as good tendencies, that the law is needed to restrain him. L.

[6] Phenomenal being is compared to the diacritical point on the letter *'ayn* (eye or essence), which converts it into the letter *ghayn* (cloud or darkness). When *'ayn* is freed from this dot, *ghayn*, the cloud of phenomenal being, is sublimated into *'ayn*, Divine Essence. L.

[7] *I.e.* (1) passing by self-annihilation (*fana*) back to Absolute Being from

The second is passing over the field of existence.
In this holy vision plurality and individuals are one,[1]
Like one which pervades all numbers.
You are that plurality which becomes very Unity[2]
You are that Unity which becomes very plurality.
A man may know this mystery when he passes forth
From the part, and travels up to the whole.

QUESTION IV.

Of what sort is this traveller, who is this wayfarer?
Of whom shall I say that he is the perfect man?

ANSWER IV.

Again you ask 'Who is the traveller on the road?'
It is he who is acquainted with his own origin.
He is a traveller who passes on with haste,
And becomes pure from self as fire from smoke.
Know his journey is a progress of revelation from the contingent
To the necessary, leading away from darkness and defect.[3]
He travels back his first journey, stage after stage,
Till he attains the grade of the perfect man.[4]

phenomenal being, and (2) enduring *(baka)* in mystical union with Absolute Being, and with Him being in turn manifested in plurality.

"They say the road is two steps, severing and uniting;
You are united to the 'Friend,' when severed from self." L.

[1] *I. e.*, In the vision of the illumined and perfected Sufi. L.

[2] In virtue of man's 'journey to God' he is plurality in Unity, and in virtue of his 'journey with God from God' he is carried down again into plurality. L.

[3] *Nuksan*, 'deficiency,' 'nothingness.' In the *Akhlaki Nasiri* (Preface), practice is defined as "exertion in action and endeavour in conduct to the utmost of human ability, with the object of developing what lies within the compass of potentiality, up to the stage of actuality, provided that it leads from defect *(nuksan)* to perfection." See *'Ayun ul Masail*, by Abu Nasir Al-Farabi, § 4. Schmölders, Documenta, p. 45.

[4] In the last answer Mahmud spoke of 'the journey up to God,' and that 'down from God with God.' Here he mentions another journey or descent, anterior to the other two, viz. that of man's first extrusion from Unity into phenomenal plurality.

RULE I.[1]

Know first how the perfect man is produced
From the time he is first engendered.
He is produced at first as inanimate matter,
Next by the added spirit he is made sentient,[2]
And acquires the motive powers from the Almighty.
Next he is made lord of will by "The Truth."
In childhood opens out perception of the world,
And the temptations of the world act upon him.[3]
When all the particular parts are ordered in him
He makes his way from these sources to general notions.[4]
Anger is born in him, and lust of the flesh,
And from these spring avarice, gluttony, pride.
Evil dispositions come into operation.
He becomes worse than an animal, a demon, a brute.
In his descent this point is the very lowest,
For it is the point directly opposite to Unity.
Of actions there arises an endless plurality,
He is thus directly opposed to his beginning.
If he remains imprisoned in this snare,
He goes astray worse than the beasts.[5]

[1] This rule, after shortly sketching man's 'descent' into the world of phenomena, describes his upward 'journey to God'—from the lowest point in the circle of being, up again to the highest point.

[2] 'Added spirit.' Lahiji doubts whether this means the animal soul or vital principle, or the human soul. This doctrine of the three ascending grades of the soul, vegetive, animal and human, was first enunciated by Aristotle, and is reproduced in the '*Ayun ul Masail* and other works. So Dryden (Palamon and Arcite, III. *sub fin.*), says that man is

> "First vegetive, then feels, and reasons last,
> Rich of three souls, and lives all three to waste."

[3] Here is another reproduction of the Aristotelian forms of thought. Though the senses existed in the fœtus in 'potentiality,' yet it is not till the world of outward objects is presented to them that they come into 'actuality.'

[4] When particular sensations and perceptions are acquired, reason deduces general notions from them. L.

[5] Koran, *Sura* VII. 178. Compare "In Memoriam," 117, 7:

> "Move upward, working out the beast,
> And let the ape and tiger die."

But if from the spirit world there shines a light
From the attraction of grace or reflection of proof,[1]
Then his heart has fellowship with the light of "The Truth,"
And he turns back along the road which he came.
From that divine attraction or certain proof
He finds his way to assured faith.
He arises from the seventh hell of the wicked,
He sets his face towards the seventh heaven of the righteous;
Then is he clothed with the quality of repentance,[2]
And is made one chosen among the children of Adam.[3]
From evil deeds he becomes pure,
Like Idris the prophet he is caught up to heaven.
When he obtains release from evil habits,
He becomes thereby like Noah a saviour of his own life.
The power of his 'parts' remains not in the 'Whole,'
And like "the Friend of God" he acquires trust in God.[4]
His will is joined with the pleasure of "The Truth,"
And like Moses he enters the highest door.
He obtains release from his own knowledge,
And like the prophet Jesus he becomes near to God,[5]
He gives up his existence utterly to be plundered,
And in the steps of the "Most Pure" he ascends.[6]
But when his last point is joined to his first,
There is no entrance for angel or for prophet.[7]

[1] *I.e.* illumination, or logical demonstration. L.

[2] *Taubat*, repentance, or returning to God, has four stages, viz. turning (1) from unbelief, (2) from evil actions, (3) from evil habits, (4) from all but God. L.

[3] See note on couplet 545.

[4] *I.e.* he attains *fana*, utter effacement and annihilation of self,—obliteration of all consciousness and perception of the external phenomenal world,—immersion of the soul in the ocean of Divine glory. This state of *fana* involves the effacement of his individual power, will, knowledge and entire existence, as set forth in this and the three following couplets. L.

[5] See Koran, *Sura* III. 40. 'He has near access to God.'

[6] *I. e.* Muhammad.

[7] Referring to the *Hadis*, quoted under couplet 120.

Illustration.[1]

The prophet is as a sun, the saint as a moon
Is set over against him in the point '*I am with God.*'
Prophethood is resplendent in its own perfection,
The saintship therein is manifest and not hidden.
But the saintship in a saint is concealed,
Whereas in a prophet it is shown forth openly.
When a saint by obedience obtains fellowship,
And intimacy with the prophet in saintship;[2]
Then from the text '*If ye love God*' he finds entrance
To that secret chamber '*God will love you.*'[3]
In that secret chamber he is beloved,
He becomes altogether 'drawn'[4] to "The Truth."
The saint is obedient as to his essence,
He is a devotee in the street of essence,[5]
Howbeit his work is finished at the time
That his end is joined again to his beginning?[6]

Answer IV.—*Continued.*

He is a perfect man who in all perfection
Does the work of a slave[7] in spite of his lordliness.

[1] Saintship, *waliyat*, *i.e.* drawing near to God by effacement of self, is common saints and prophets; but while prophets have to preach, saints have only to ey. L.

[2] As an intimate, *muhrim*, he obtains entrance to the *haram*.

[3] Koran, *Sura* III. 29.

[4] *Majzub i mutlak* is the appellation of the Sufi in the stage of *fana*.

[5] Though absorbed in "The Truth" he is still obedient as regards his essence, cause by obedience he attained his exaltation. L.

[6] Here 'beginning' means the state of phenomenal existence, and 'end' the state absorption in the Absolute. The saint first accomplishes 'the journey to God,' ding in absorption (*fana*) and abiding or eternal life in God (*baka*), and then urneys down again to his beginning in the 'journey from God along with God,' d is conscious that he is Unity in plurality. L.

[7] Servitude, obedience, *'abudiyat*, is the characteristic quality of a saint.—Shea's *abistan*, III. 241, note. In his downward journey the saint must observe and obey e positive law, notwithstanding his previous union with Allah. L.

Afterwards, when he has finished his course,
"The Truth" sets on his head the crown of Khalifate.[1]
He finds eternal life after dying to self, and again
He runs another course from his end to his beginning.
He makes the law his upper garment,
He makes the mystic path his inner garment.
But know very truth is the station of his nature,
He comprehends both infidelity and faith.
Being endued with fair virtues,
And famed for knowledge, devotion and piety,
All these in him, but he far from all these,
Overshadowed beneath the canopy of Divine Epiphanies.[2]

ILLUSTRATION.[3]

The kernel of an almond is utterly spoiled,
If you pluck it from its husk while it is unripe.
But when it grows ripe in its husk, it is good;
If you pluck out its kernel, you break the husk.
The law is the husk, and the truth is the kernel,
The mystic path lies between this and that.
Error in the traveller's path is spoiling of the kernel,
When the kernel is ripe it is good without its husk.
When the knower experiences certain assurance,[4]
The kernel becomes ripe, and bursts the husk.
His being remains not in this world,
He departs, and returns again no more.
Another shines as a bright sun still retaining the husk,[5]

[1] *I.e.* the vicegerence of God on earth. Koran, *Sura* II. 28: "Verily we ar about to place one on earth as a Khalif."

[2] *I.e.* He is in the state of *fana*, or absorption in God, like Moses at Moun Sinai. Koran, *Sura* VII. 139, quoted in note to couplet 194.

[3] This illustration is explanatory of the distinction of law, *shari'at*, the Suf course, *tarikat*, and truth, *hakikat*, all of which go to form the perfect man. L.

[4] Knower, *i. e.* he who obtains Divine 'illumination.' L.

[5] One class rest at the stage of *fana*, ecstatic absorption in Unity, and law has no more dominion over them. These are the "*Majzub i Mutlak, Azad* or *Be Shara*'" devotees. Another, more perfect class, pass on to the stage of 'sobriety after

When in this state he makes another circuit.
From water and earth he springs up into a tree,
Whose branches are lifted up above the heavens.[1]
The same brings forth in his turn another seed,
One yielding a hundred fold by fiat of the Almighty.
Like the growth of a seed into the line of a tree,
From point comes a line, and from line again a circle.
When the pilgrim has finished the circuit of this circle,
Then his last point is joined to his first.
Again he may be likened to a pair of compasses,
Ending in the same impression whence they began.[2]
When he has finished his course to the end,
"The Truth" sets on his head the crown of Khalifate.
These circuits are not transmigrations of souls, for verily
They are manifested in the visions of Epiphanies,[3]
'Verily they ask, saying, what is the end,
And the answer is the return to the beginning.'[4]

Rule II.[5]

The first appearance of prophethood was in Adam,
And its perfection was in the 'Seal of the prophets.'[6]

ntoxication,' and carrying with them "The Truth," descend to phenomenal being, and n that descent fulfil all the duties of the law as an ensample to others. L.

[1] "The Truth," like a kernel or seed embodied in the 'knower,' comes down as a hining light or pattern to the phenomenal world, though still retaining the husk of he law. This seed is sown in the good soil of his disciples, and springs upon hem into a tree, which again is lifted up to heaven, *i. e.* repeats the same circuit ıp to Allah. L.

[2] Obeying the law in his downward journey, as he did in his first upward journey. L.

[3] In metempsychosis one body perishes and another succeeds it as a receptacle of he soul, but in these circuits the truth may be manifested in teacher and disciple t once. L.

[4] See Koran, *Sura* LVII. 6: "And unto God shall all things return." And X. 4: "He produceth a creature, and then causeth it to return again." Compare the *Proodos* and *Epistrophe* of Proclus, the raying out and return of all existences from nd to the absolute unity. Ueberweg, History of Philosophy, Eng. Trans. I. 257.

[5] On the relation of prophethood to saintship, the two embodiments of truth, *hakikat.*

[6] Muhammad.

Saintship lingers behind while it makes a journey,
And like a point makes another circuit in the world.[1]
Its entirety will be seen in the 'Seal of the saints,'
In him will be completed the circuit of the world.[2]
Individual saints are as it were his members,
For he is the whole and they are the parts.
Since he holds close relation to our lord,
Through him will be shown mercy most complete.[3]
He will be the Imam of both worlds,
He will be the Khalif of the children of Adam.

Illustration.[4]

When the light of the sun is divided from the night,
You see its dawn and up-rising and full ascension.
Again from the circling of the revolving heavens
Declension and afternoon and sunset are seen.
The light of the prophet is a mighty sun,[5]
Now shining in Moses, now in Adam.
If you read the chronicles of the world,
You will know clearly its several degrees.
From this sun every moment is cast a shadow,
Which is one degree in the ascension of faith.
The time of our lord is the meridian line,[6]
For he is purified from all shadow of darkness.
On the meridian line he stands upright,

[1] When prophecy ceased with Muhammad, saintship alone remained, and made the circuit of the world in the persons of the various saints. L.

[2] Muhammad Mehdi, the twelfth Imam, who will appear at the end of the world.

[3] Koran, *Sura* XXI. 107: "We have not sent thee, but as a mercy to all creatures."

[4] On the relation of the minor prophets to Muhammad, and the minor saints to Muhammad Mehdi. L.

[5] *I.e.* Muhammad. He is said to be *Ruh i 'azam*, *'Akl i kull*, and *hakikat i insani*, that is, the first emanation from Deity; and the minor prophets are thus emanations from him. Hence he is compared to the Sun, because 'the first thing God emitted was light.' L.

[6] When the sun is on the meridian, at the time of the equinox, there are no shadows in countries near the Equator. L. Compare Dante, Purgatorio, XXX. 89.

Casting no shadow before or behind, on the right hand or on the left.
Since he stands on the '*narrow way*' "of The Trûth,"[1]
And takes his stand on the command '*Be steadfast.*'[2]
He casts no shadow, for that involves darkness.
Hail, O Light of God, O shadow of Divinity!
His *Kibla*[3] is between east and west,
Because it is drowned in the midst of light.
When by his power Satan becomes a Musulman,[4]
He will be as a shadow hidden under his feet.
All degrees are beneath his degree,
The existence of things of earth is from his shadow.
From his light his saintship is casting shadows,
The west is made equal to the east.[5]
For every shadow cast at the beginning of his course,
Another corresponding one is cast at the ending.
At this present every doctor of the faith
Is as one corresponding to the prophets in prophecy.[6]
But since a prophet is most perfect through prophethood,
He is of necessity more excellent than any saint.
Saintship will be all shown forth in the "Seal of the Saints;"
The last point will be finished in the first.
Through him the earth will be filled with peace and faith,

[1] Koran, *Sura* I. 3. The allusion is to the *Sirat*, or narrow bridge over hell, along hich all men will have to pass on the day of judgment.

[2] "Be thou steadfast therefore as thou hast been commanded." — Koran, *ura* XI. 114.

[3] *Kibla*, the point to which the faithful turn in prayer, indicated by the *Mihrab*, niche in mosques. See Daniel vi. 10. Lahiji says the *Kibla* of Moses was in e West, and that of Jesus in the East, but that of Muhammad in the centre.

[4] There is a tradition, both among the Muhammadans and in the Kabbala, that tan will become an angel of light. Compare 2 Cor. xi. 14.

[5] The lesser prophets and saints are reflections from his light. The reflections ring the ascent of the Sun of prophecy up to Muhammad are prophets, and those ring its descent saints, who are also prophets in one sense. L.

[6] Alluding to the *Hadis*: "The *'ulama* of my faith are as the prophets of the ildren of Israel."

Through him stones and animals will receive life.[1]
There will remain not in the world one infidel soul,
True equity will be made manifest altogether.
By the secret of Unity he will attain to "The Truth,"
In him will be shown forth the face of the "Absolute."[2]

QUESTION V.

Who then is he who attains to the secret of unity?
Who is the understanding one that is a knower?[3]

ANSWER V.

That man attains to the secret of unity
Who is not detained at the stages on the road.
But the knower is he that knows Very Being,
He that witnesses Absolute Being.[4]
He recognises no being but Very Being,
And being such as his own he gambles clean away.
Your being is naught but thorns and weeds,[5]
Cast it all clean away from you.
Go sweep out the chamber of your heart,

[1] With this may be compared the eulogium on the prophet in the introduction o the *Mantik ut Tair*. See Garcin de Tassy ("Poesie Philosophique et Religieuse,' p. 24). Muhammad Mehdi is Muhammad in his second coming. L.

[2] Koran, *Sura* XXVIII. 88: "Everything perishes except Thy face."

[3] Knower, one who beholds "The Truth" with his 'illumined' soul, and no with his reason. The 'secret of Unity' is that there is no other being besides "Th Truth." L.

[4] Absolute Being is that which is free from all limitation, *kaid*. L.

[5] Compare Hafiz, Ode 385 (Brockhaus' edition):

"Sweep off the life of Hafiz as a dream,
Whilst Thou art, none shall hear me say 'I am.'"

And Ode 487:

"From His heart girdle-wise you dwell apart,
While girdle-wise your 'self' enfolds your heart."

Make it ready to be the dwelling-place of the Beloved.
When you depart out, He will enter in,
In you, void of your*self*, will He display His beauty.
The man who is loved for his '*pious works*,[1]
Whom the pains of 'negation'[2] purify as a room that is swept,
He finds an abode in a '*laudable station*,'
He finds a portion in '*what eye hath not seen, nor ear heard.*'[3]
But while the stain of his own being remains on him,
The knowledge of the knower assumes not the form of experience.[4]
Until you cast away obstacles from before you,
The light enters not the chamber of your heart.
As there are four obstacles in this world,
So also the modes of purification from them are four:[5]
First, purification from filthiness of the flesh;
Second, from sin and evil "*whispers of the tempter*;"[6]
The third is the purification from bad habits,
Which make men as beasts of the field;
The fourth is the purification of the secret,[7]
For at this point the pilgrim's journeyings cease.
Whoso is cleansed with these purifications,
Verily he is fit to commune with God.

[1] "And watch some part of the night in the same exercise as a pious work of pererogation for thee, peradventure thy Lord will raise thee to a laudable station." Koran, *Sura* XVII. 81.

[2] In the ejaculation "*zikr*" of the creed, *kalima*, ('There is no God but God, and uhammad is the prophet of God'), the first clause is called negation, *nafi*. Here egation' means denying all other existences besides God. L. The expression *ains* of negation' would also seem to imply self-denial in a practical sense,— ortifying the flesh.

[3] See 1 Corinthians ii. 9.

[4] See couplet 63. His theoretical knowledge is naught, till he personally experiences d feels the 'Secret of Unity.' L.

[5] These are the four degrees of purification enumerated by Ghazzali.—Sale's Koran, elim. Discourse, 75.

[6] Koran, *Sura* CXIV. 4.

[7] "Secret," *i. e.* the heart, the secret thoughts. L.

Until you utterly gamble away yourself,[1]
How can your prayer be true prayer?[2]
When your essence is pure from all stain,[3]
Then it is that your prayers are '*a joy of the eyes,*'[4]
There remains then no distinction,
Knower and known are one and the same.

QUESTION VI.

If knower and known are both the One pure essence,
What are the aspirations in this handful of dust?[5]

ANSWER VI.

Be not thankless for the grace of "The Truth,"
For it is by the light of "The Truth" that you know "The Truth:"[6]

[1] From the harvest of existence he will never reap a grain
Who has never sown a seed corn in annihilation's lane.
Hafiz (Brockhaus' edition), Ode 61.

[2] Ghazzali, quoted in Tholuck, Ssufismus, pp. 4. 105, says, "Prayers (*zikr*) have three veils, (1) prayers pronounced with the tongue only, (2) prayers undistracted by evil thoughts, (3) prayers offered with such fervour, that the mind can hardly be recalled from thoughts of God. But the marrow of prayer is when the object of prayer possesses the heart, and prayer is effaced and ceases, and the sayer of prayer attends no more to prayer nor his own heart. These are submerged, and if he attends to them that is a veil and a distraction. This is the state named *fana*, effacement, wherein he is effaced from self, so that he is aware neither of his body, nor of outward things, nor of inward affections. He is 'rapt' from all these, journeying first *to* his Lord, second *in* his Lord: and if the thought that he is effaced from self occurs to him, that is a blemish. The best stage is to be effaced from effacement." Compare St. Theresa's 'Prayer of Rapture.'—Vaughan, II. 132.

[3] *I. e.* stain of your own phenomenal individual being, or self. L. This is just Eckart's view. Vaughan, I. 163.

[4] Koran, *Sura* XXXII. 18.

[5] What is the cause of the love and ardour for knowledge of "The Truth" seen in man? L.

[6] Having no real existence of your own, it is only by the communicated existence and knowledge of God that you know Him. L.

Besides Him is no knower or known, Be sure,
Nevertheless the dust draws heat from the sun.[1]
It is not strange that the motes of dust have hope,[2]
And desire for the sun's heat and light.
Call to mind the state and circumstance of your creation,
For thence will you learn the root of your thought.
To whom said God, '*Am not I your Lord?*'[3]
Who was it who then answered '*Yea?*'
On that day when He '*kneaded the clay,*'[4]
He wrote by grace the faith on the heart.
If you will read forthwith that writing,[5]
You will understand whatsoever you desire.
Last night you tied the knot of the "covenant of service,"[6]
But have now forgotten it through ignorance;
And therefore the word of "The Truth" was sent down[7]
To recall to your mind that primeval covenant.
If you have seen "The Truth" at the beginning,
You may see Him again in this place.
In this place behold His attributes to-day,
That you may behold His essence to-morrow.[8]

[1] Just as man draws his ardour for knowledge of "The Truth," from "The Truth." L.

[2] Motes are only seen in the sunbeams, just as the phenomena men are manifested by the shining of "The Truth." L.

[3] "And when the Lord drew forth their posterity from the loins of Adam, and took them to witness against themselves, saying, Am not I your Lord? they answered, Yea."—Koran, *Sura* VII. 171. Knowledge of God was thus one of the essential properties implanted in man at his first origin. L.

[4] Alluding to the *Hadis*: "He kneaded the clay of Adam forty days."

[5] *I.e.* the innate knowledge engraved on the heart at creation. L.

[6] The creature when fresh from the Divine hand, undefiled by plurality, knew and confessed its dependence on "The Truth." L.

[7] *I.e.* in the mouths of the prophets.

[8] *I.e.* in the world to come. This is addressed only to ordinary men, for saints and 'knowers' attain the world to come in this present world. L.

And if you cannot, yet be not cast down,
Go, hearken to the text '*Thou canst not direct.*'[1]

ILLUSTRATION.[2]

He that is born blind believes not what you say of colours,
Though you show him instances and proofs for a century.
White and yellow and red and dark and light green
Are to him naught but darkest black.
See the evil plight of one blind from his birth,
Can he ever gain sight from the physician's eye salve?
Reason cannot see the state of the world to come,
As a man born blind cannot see things in this world.
But in addition to reason man has a certain faculty,[3]
Whereby he perceives hidden mysteries.
Like fire in flint and steel,
God has placed this faculty in man's soul and body;
When that flint and steel are struck together,[4]
The two worlds are illumined by the flash!
From that collision is this mystery made clear,
Now you have heard it, go and attend to your Self.

[1] "Verily thou canst not direct whom thou wilt, but God directeth whom he pleaseth."—Koran, *Sura* XXVIII. 56. It is not every one who has power to see and know "The Truth" in this life. L.

[2] Those who are void of the capacity for knowledge of God, and who are not 'illumined' by Divine grace, are like men born blind. The religious faculty is wanting in them. They have nothing but reason to rely on. L.

[3] 'Faculty,' *taur*, literally mode, manner, condition, state, action. It is evoked, says Lahiji, by love and desire of knowledge of "The Truth," and ends, when exposed to the favourable conditions of the Sufi 'progress,' in Divine illumination. The leading principle of all mysticism is that independently of reason man possesses an inward sense or faculty—an 'inner light,' or an intuition, which under certain conditions conveys to him a knowledge of God by direct apprehension, in a manner similar to the evidence of the senses. Hugo of St. Victor names it the 'Eye of Intelligence.'—Vaughan, I. 134.

[4] The striking together of the flint and steel means the Sufi progress, the purifying the heart from the stain of 'other.' By this collision the flame of love is kindled which burns up the Sufi's phenomenal being, and shows him his true 'self' an integral portion of "The All." L.

Your Self is a copy made in the image of God,[1]
Seek in your Self all that you desire to know.[2]

QUESTION VII.

To what point belongs the aphorism, '*I am The Truth?*'[3]
Why call you that impostor a vain babbler?[4]

ANSWER VII.

Verily '*I am The Truth*' is a revelation of absolute mystery,
Save 'The Truth,' who can say '*I am The Truth?*'
All the atoms of the world, like Mansur,
You will take to be drunken and heavy with wine;
Continually are they singing this song of praise,[5]
Continually dwelling on this mystic verity.
If you desire that its meaning may be clear to you,
Then read the text, '*All praise Allah.*'[6]
When you have carded 'self' as cotton,

[1] Similarly, Bernard of Clairvaux taught that each soul contains a copy of the ideas in the Divine mind, so that the pure in heart, in proportion as they have cleansed the internal mirror, must in knowing themselves also know God.—Vaughan, I. 34. Compare the *Hadis*: "He created Adam in His own image," and, "He who knows himself knows his Lord." L.

[2] *I.e.* in your real self, after you have died to your phenomenal self, and live eternally again in "The Truth." Compare Max Müller, Hibbert Lectures, 375. "The (Brahman's) highest knowledge was expressed in the words *tat tvam*, 'thou art It'; thou thyself, thy own true Self, that which can never be taken from thee; when everything else that seemed to be thine for a time disappears; when all that was created vanishes again like a dream, thy own true Self belongs to the Eternal Self; the Atman or Self within thee is the true Brahman, from whom thou wast estranged for a time through birth and death, but who receives thee back again as soon as thou returnest to Him or to It."

[3] Point, *i.e.* the point or degree of the Mystic who has found eternal life in real Unity after annihilation of his phenomenal self, *baka ba'd ul fana*. L.

[4] Hossain Mansur 'Hallaj' (the wool-carder), who was put to death at Bagdad in 309 A. H. for using these words.

[5] *Tahlil* and *Tasbih* are two of the ejaculations in most frequent use.

[6] "There is naught but praiseth Allah."—Koran, *Sura* XVII. 46.

You, like the 'wool carder,' will raise this cry.
Take out the cotton of your illusion from your ears,
Hearken to the call of *The One, The Almighty.*[1]
This call is ever coming to you from "The Truth,"
Why are you tarrying for the last day?
Come into the "valley of peace," for straightway[2]
The bush will say to you, '*Verily I am Allah.*'
The saying "*I am 'The Truth'*" was lawful for the bush,
Why is it unlawful in the mouth of a good man?
Every man whose heart is pure from doubt,
Knows for a surety that there is no being but 'One.'
Saying 'I am' belongs only to "The Truth,"
For essence is absent, and illusive appearance is absent.[3]
The glory of "The Truth" admits no duality,
In that glory is no 'I' or 'We' or 'Thou.'
'I,' 'We,' 'Thou' and 'He' are all one thing,
For in Unity there is no distinction of persons.
Every man who as a void is empty of self,
Re-echoes within him the cry '*I am The Truth;*'
He takes his eternal side, 'other' perishes,[4]
Travelling, travel, and traveller all become One.
Incarnation and Communion spring from 'other,'
But very Unity comes from the mystic journey.[5]
That which is separate from "The Truth" is phenomenal
existence,

[1] "With whom shall be the power on that day? With God, the One, the Almighty."—Koran, *Sura* XL. 16.

[2] See Koran, *Sura* XX. 14, for the history of the burning bush.

[3] Essence, literally "He," *Hu*, which is the technical name of metaphysical essence in regard of its hidden nature. L. Aristotle, Met. VII. (VI.) 10, says, matter in itself is incognoscible.

[4] Every existing thing has two 'sides' or aspects, one *quâ* its phenomenal being which is 'other,' and one *quâ* its real being, as an integral portion of 'Unity,' which is its eternal side. L.

[5] *I. e.* the annihilation of man's phenomenal self, which obscures his real Self, 'The Truth,' as the waves cover the sea. L.

Neither does "The Truth" become a creature, nor is a
creature united with Allah.[1]
Incarnation and Communion are here impossible,[2]
For duality in unity is clearly absurd.
The existence of creatures and plurality is but a semblance,
And not every thing that seems to be really is.

ILLUSTRATION.[3]

Set a mirror over against you,[4]
Look on it and see that other person.
Again see what that reflection is,
It is not this nor that, what then is that reflection?
Since I am limited to my own proper self,
I know not what is this shadow of me;
In fine, how can not being be joined with being?
The two, light and darkness, cannot be united.
Like the past the future month and year exist not,
What is there but this one point of the present?
Time is one imaginary point, and that ever passing away,
You have named it the fleeting river.
There is none other in this desert, but only I,
Tell me what is this echo and noise?
Accidents are fleeting, substance is compounded of them,
Say how does it exist or where is this compound?[5]
Bodies exist only through length, breadth and depth,

[1] As in Incarnation and Communion. L.

[2] *Hulul*, Incarnation, as in couplet 102. *Ittihad*, the conjunction or communion of two *different* things or persons in one. *Wahdat*, unity, oneness. See Tholuck, Ssufismus, page 142. There were sects of Sufis who held each of these doctrines.—Malcolm's Persia, II. 271.

[3] This illustration gives samples of apparent existences, which are not really existent, *e.g.* reflections, past and future time, echoes, and even substances (bodies), since they are composed only of fleeting accidents. L.

[4] Hugo of St. Victor uses the same illustration.—Maurice, Mediæval Philosophy, page 145.

[5] See couplet 478.

Since their existence proceeds from these nonentities.[1]
And of this kind is all the fabric of the two worlds;
Now you know this, have faith and be stablished.
Of a truth there is no other existence than "The Truth,"
Whether you say '*He is the Truth*,' or '*I am the Truth*.'
Separate imaginary appearances from True Being,
Make not yourself a stranger but a friend.[2]

QUESTION VIII.

Why call they a creature 'united,'[3]
How can he achieve travelling and journey?

ANSWER VIII.

Union with "The Truth" is separation from the creature state,[4]
Friendship with Him is estrangement from self.[5]
When the contingent wipes off the dust of contingency,
Nothing remains save Necessary Being.
The existence of the two worlds is as a dream,
In the moment of eternity they become naught.
He who is 'united' is not a creature,[6]
The perfect man says not so.
How shall not being find entrance at that door?
What connection has the dust with the Lord of Lords?

[1] *I.e.* the accidents of length, breadth and depth. L.

[2] It is only these phenomenal appearances, which are mere accidental accretions to True Being, that veil it from you, and make you a stranger to it. L.

[3] This answer discusses the nature of the perfected Sufi, ***wasil i Hakk***, *i.e.* he who has drawn near to "The Truth,"—who has arrived at Unity. ***Wasal*** is defined in the ***Tamámi-ul-asámi***, "The extinction of our own existence in the existence of God, as snow melts in the sea and as motes vanish in the sun."—Tholuck, Ssufismus, 72. Compare the ***Henosis*** and ***Haplosis*** of Plotinus. Ueberweg, i. 251.

[4] 'Creature state,' *i.e.* phenomenal illusion of duality. L.

[5] Compare St. James, iv. 4: "The friendship of the world is enmity with God."

[6] His phenomenal 'side' vanishes, and nothing remains but his eternal 'side' of Very Being. L.

How can not being be united with "The Truth?"
How can not being achieve travelling and journey?
If your soul were cognizant of this mystery,
You would straightway say "*God pardon my error.*[1]"
You are non-existent,[2] and not being is ever immovable,
How can this non-existent contingent move to the necessary?
No substance possesses objectivity[3] without accidents,
And what is an accident?—what "*endures not two moments.*"
Philosophers, who have written on natural science,
Define bodies by length, breadth and depth.[4]
What then is matter but an absolute nonentity
Wherein is demonstrated form?
As then form without matter is not self existent,[5]
So too matter without a form is naught but not being.
All the bodies in the universe consist of these two nonentities,
Whereof nothing is known, but their non-existence.
Consider then their whole essence without more or less,[6]
In itself it is neither existent nor non-existent.[7]
Look upon contingent being in spirit and in truth,
For apart from necessary being it is naught.
Absolute Being by its own perfection is pervading all,[8]
Phenomenal objects are mere imaginary things;[9]
Imaginary things are not really existent,

[1] *I.e.* in calling a creature 'united,' *Wasil i Hakk.* L.

[2] *I.e.* in your creature state. L.

[3] 'Objectivity,' *'ayn*,—evidence, visibility, externality. "Non incurrunt ipsæ substantiæ in oculos, sed vestitæ et ornatæ accidentibus."—Melancthon, quoted by Hamilton, Metaphysics, I. 139.

[4] *I.e.* by mere accidents. L.

[5] See note on couplet 704.

[6] Whole essence, *mahiyat*, the Aristotelian *to ti*, species. Schmölders, Documenta. Here matter *plus* form.

[7] If existent it could not become non-existent, and *vice versa*. L.

[8] Its perfection is to be manifested. L. See couplet 139.

[9] *Amri 'itibari.* "That which has no existence except in the mind of him who conceives it, and so long as he conceives it."—*Jorjani, T'arifat*, Notices des Mss. X. 84. *I.e.* merely subjective.

Though the numbers are many, only One is counted.
The world has only a simulated existence,
Its state is but an insubstantial pageant and a farce.[1]

ILLUSTRATION.

OF MODES OF BEING.[2]

The mist is raised up out of the sea,
By command of "The Truth" it rains down on the desert.
The sun's rays are shed down from the fourth heaven,
And are mingled with the water.
Then the heat strives to ascend on high,
And the water of the sea clings to it.
And when with these are joined earth and air,
There comes forth the green and pleasant plant.[3]
This becomes the food of and is transformed into animals,
Which are eaten by and transmuted into man.
It becomes seed, and passes through divers states,
And then there is born of it another man.
Then when the reasonable soul as a light enters the body,[4]
There is produced a fair and brilliant form;
It becomes child, youth, adult and then aged man,
It knows wisdom, knowledge, reason, counsel.

[1] Compare Koran, *Sura* XXIX. 64: "This present life is no other than a pastime and a sport."

[2] *I.e.* of the modes in which Absolute Being is evolved or manifested in phenomenal plural objects. L.

[3] Compare Milton's Paradise Lost, V. 479:

So from the root
Springs lighter the green stalk, from thence the leaves
More airy, last the bright consummate flower
Spirits odorous breathes; flowers and their fruit,
Man's nourishment, by gradual scale sublimed
To *vital* spirits aspire, to *animal*,
To *intellectual*, give both life and sense
Fancy and understanding, whence the soul
Reason receives, and reason is her being.

[4] Alluding to Koran, *Sura* XV. 29: "I have breathed of my spirit into man."

Then comes his appointed time from the pure presence,
Pure spirit returns to spirit, dust to dust.[1]
All the parts of the world are like plants,
They are single drops from the ocean of life.[2]
When the set times of their manifestations pass by,
Their end becomes again their beginning.[3]
Every one of them tends towards its Centre,
For its nature forsakes not its centripetal character.
Unity is like a sea, albeit a sea of blood,[4]
Whereout rise thousands of mad waves.
Behold how this drop of water from that sea,
Has assumed so many names and forms!
Mist, cloud, rain, dew, clay,
Plant and animal, and perfect man.
In fine it was one drop of water at the first,
Wherefrom all these things were fashioned.[5]
This universe of reason, soul, heavens and bodies,[6]
Is as a drop of water in its beginning and ending.
When their appointed time comes to heaven and stars,
Their being is lost in not being.[7]
When a wave strikes it, the world vanishes away,
Then is fulfilled the text "*It abounded not yesterday.*"[8]

[1] Eccles. xii. 7.

[2] Single because each manifests one Divine Name. L. See couplet 278.

[3] They all end in the 'sea of Unity.' L.

[4] It is a sea of blood because of the continual annihilation in it of its waves, *viz.* phenomena and plurality. L.

[5] Compare Wisdom xi. 23; and Koran, *Sura* XXI. 31: "We made every living thing of water."

[6] Reason *i.e.* Universal Reason, the first Emanation, as in couplet 204. L.

[7] The Koranic texts about the last day are applied by the Sufis to the continual annihilation of phenomena in Unity. L.

[8] "Verily the likeness of this present life is no other than as water, which we send down from heaven, and wherewith the produce of the earth is mixed, of which men eat and cattle also until the earth hath received its vesture and is adorned. The inhabitants thereof imagine that they have power over the same, but our command cometh unto it by night or by day, and we render it mown, as though yesterday it had not abounded with fruits."—Koran, *Sura* X. 25.

In a moment this world passes away,
None remains in the house save "The Truth."
At that moment you attain proximity,
You stripped of 'self' are 'united' to "The Beloved."
Union here means the cessation of this dream,
When this dream passes away, it is union.
Say not 'the contingent outsteps its limits,'[1]
Contingent becomes not necessary, nor necessary contingent.
He who is transcendent in spiritual mysteries,
Says not this, for it is an inversion of verities.
O master! you have a thousand 'processes' before you,[2]
Go and consider your own coming and going.
Of the argument of part and whole and the 'process' of man,
I tell you every whit both manifest and secret.

QUESTION IX.

What is the union of necessary and contingent?
What are 'near' and 'far,' 'more' and 'less'?[3]

ANSWER IX.

Hear of me a discourse without 'more' or 'less,'
It is by nearness that you become far from your*self*.
As Being is manifested in not being,
From that too proceed 'near' and 'far,' 'more' and 'less.'[4]

[1] *I.e.* not being. L.

[2] *Nisha.* Lahiji says this includes the processes of *mubda*, coming or origin, *ma'ash*, sustenance, and *mu'ad*, return or going. Compare Koran, *Sura* XXIX. 17: "See how Allah originated the creature world, and then created a new creation."

[3] Union having already been explained, the poet passes at once to the explanation of 'near' and 'far.' "We are nearer to Him than his neck vein." — Koran, *Sura* L. 15. L.

[4] 'More' of Being is reflected in the man who is nearest to "The Light." L.

He is 'near' on whom '*the light is shed,*'[1]
'Far' is that not being which is distant from Being;
If He makes to shine on you a light from Himself,
It delivers you from your own existence.
What profit to you is there in this non-existent existence,
Whence you have now fear and now hope?
As man fears not him whom he knows,
It is infants who are frightened at shadows.
Fear remains not when you have started on your journey,[2]
The Arab racer needs not the whip.
What fear will you have of the fires of hell,
When your soul and body are purged from existence?
Let pure gold be burned in the fire,
If it contains no alloy, what is there to burn?
There is no obstacle in your way but your*self*,
But reflect well on your own illusory existence,
While you are cloaked in this self of yours,
The world is always as a veil before your eyes.
Then you are the lowest part of the circle of being,
Then are you most opposed to the point of unity;[3]
The phenomena of the world overpower you,[4]
Thence like Satan you say "Who is like unto me?"
Thence you say "I myself have free-will,"
"My body is the horse and my soul the rider,"
"The reins of the body are in the hand of the soul,"
"The entire direction thereof is given to me."
Know you not that all this is the road of the Magians,[5]

[1] Alluding to the *Hadis*: "God formed the creation in darkness, then He shed His light thereon, and he whom it meets is guided in the right way, and he who misses it walketh in darkness."

[2] He who has started on the 'journey to God' is engrossed in his race. L.

[3] Compare couplet 324.

[4] All the attributes of God, egoism included, are manifested as phenomena in man. Hence pride, like Satan's. "I am nobler than he."—Koran, *Sura* VII. 77.

[5] Alluding to the *Hadis*: "The men of freewill are Guebers." They set up man's will beside God's, like Ahriman beside Ormuzd. Koran, *Sura* XXII. 17. "If man

All these lies and deception come from illusive existence?
530 How, O foolish man, can free-will appertain
To a person whose essence is nothingness?
Seeing that your being is all one with not being,
Say whence comes this free-will of yours?
A man whose real existence is not of himself,
Is neither good nor evil in his own essence.[1]
Whom have you seen in the whole world
Who ever once acquired pleasure without pain?
Who in fine ever attained all his desires?
Who continued ever at his pitch of perfection?[2]
535 Dignities are permanent, but men of dignity
Are subject to the sway of "The Truth." *Allah is over all.*
Recognise the "*working*"[3] of "The Truth" in every place,
Place not foot beyond your own proper limits.
Ask of your own state what this free-will is,
And thence know who are the men of free-will.
Every man whose faith is other than predestinarian,
Is according to the prophet even as a Gueber.
Like as those Guebers speak of Yezdan and Aherman,
So these ignorant fools say 'I' and 'He.'
540 The attribution of actions to us is imaginary,
That attribution itself is but a play and a farce.
You existed not when your actions were originated,
You were appointed to fulfil a certain purpose.[4]

be a self-determining agent, will it not necessarily follow that there are as many first causes as there are men in the world?"—Toplady, VI. 31.

[1] Qualities and will flow from essence, and where there is no essence there are no qualities. L.

[2] Lahiji explains the argument to be that, if man's will were free, nothing would impede the fulfilment of all his wishes. Compare Anwari:

"If destiny be not the arbiter of mundane affairs,
"Wherefore are men's states contrary to their wishes?"

[3] Alluding to the *Hadis*: "In existence there is none who works but God." And to Koran, *Sura* LV. 29. Compare John v. 17.

[4] Lahiji says this was to reflect the being, qualities, and names of God as a polished mirror, not that man should choose the actions most pleasing to himself.

By the uncaused sovereign will of "The Truth,"
By His fore-knowledge giving absolute command,
There was predestined, before soul and body were,
For every man his appointed work;
One was obedient for seven hundred thousand years,[1]
Yet afterwards bore the collar of curses on his neck.
Another after his transgression beheld the pure light,
When he repented, he obtained the name "*Chosen;*"[2]
And, more marvellous still, it was by Satan's disobedience
That Adam received mercy and pardon from "The Truth,"[3]
Whilst through Adam's sin Satan was cursed.
O wondrous actions of Thine without how or why!
The Divine Majesty '*regards not,*'[4]
Exalted high above fanciful reasonings.
How came it, O foolish man, that from eternity
This man was to be Muhammad, and that Abu Jahl?[5]
He who speaks of how and why in connection with God
Like a polytheist speaks unworthily of His Majesty.
It becomes Him to ask how and why,
Cavils on the part of His slaves are unbecoming.
Godship consists entirely in sovereignty.[6]
Causation is inapplicable to the acts of God,
Mercy and vengeance befit Godship;

[1] Iblis, or Satan.

[2] Adam. "Above all men did God choose Adam."—Koran, *Sura* III. 30.

[3] These are instances of the inscrutable nature of the Divine will, which is not determined by ascertainable causes. Satan's original obedience and Adam's disobedience went for naught. L. See Rom. xi. 33.

[4] Alluding to the *Hadis*: "These are in heaven, and God regards not their sins, and these in hell, and God regards not their good works."

[5] Abu Jahl, 'the father of folly,' was an inveterate enemy of Muhammad.—Koran, *Sura* XXII.

[6] "God was the First Great Cause, His will the source of all things, the spring of all motions, all events: it could not be frustrated." This was contained in the very idea of Omnipotence and Divine Felicity, for no perfect agency can be impeded. Aquinas, cited in Mozley, Augustinian Doctrine of Predestination, 237. Compare Aristotle, Nicom. Eth. VII. 13.

But slaveship lies in poverty and necessity,
The '*honour*' of man lies in being under compulsion,[1]
Not in having a share in free-will.
Man has nothing whatever of himself,
Yet God asks him concerning good and evil.[2]
Man has no free-will, but is under compulsion:
Ah, poor creature, seeming to be free, yet a slave!
This is not injustice, but true fore-knowledge and justice;
This is not oppression, but pure mercy and grace.
He has imposed on you the law for this cause,
That He has imparted to you of His essence.[3]
Since you are impotent in the hands of "The Truth,"
Abandon and forsake this self of yours.
In "The All" you will obtain deliverance from self,
In "The Truth" you will become rich, O Durvesh![4]
Go, Soul of your father! yield yourself to God's will,
Resign yourself to the Divine fore-ordinance.

QUESTION X.

What is that sea whose shore is speech?
What is that pearl which is found in its depths?

ANSWER X.

Being is the sea, speech is the shore,
The shells are letters, the pearls knowledge of the heart.[5]

[1] "And we have honoured the sons of Adam."—Koran, *Sura* XVII. 72.

[2] Another instance of the inscrutable nature of God's actions. L.

[3] See note on couplet 264. Being under constraint is a necessary consequence of man's acceptance of the 'burden' of displaying the Divine attributes—a penalty of his exaltation. L.

[4] When 'united' with "The Truth" you will see the Divine will working in your true Self. L.

[5] Being is a sea whereof phenomenal manifestations are the waves; speech is the shore, because speech, *logos proforikos*, is the differentia of man (animal rationale),

In every wave it casts up a thousand royal pearls
Of traditions and holy sayings and texts.
Every moment a thousand waves rise out of it,[1]
Yet it never becomes less by one drop.
Knowledge has its being from that sea,
The coverings of its pearls are voice and letters.[2]
Since mysteries are here shown in an allegory,
It is necessary to have recourse to illustrations.

Illustration.

I have heard that in the month Nysan
The pearl oysters rise to the surface of the sea of 'Umán.
From the lowest depths of the sea they come up,
And rest on the surface with opened mouths.
The mist is lifted up from the sea,
And descends in rain at the command of "The Truth."
There fall some drops into each shell's mouth,
And each mouth is shut as by a hundred bonds.
Then each shell descends into the depths with full heart,
And each drop of rain becomes a pearl.
The diver goes down to the depths of the sea,
And thence brings up the glittering pearls.
The shore is your body, the sea is Being,[3]
The mist Grace,[4] the rain knowledge of the Names.[5]
The diver of this mighty sea is human reason,
Who holds a hundred pearls wrapped in his cloth.
The heart is to knowledge as a vessel,
The shells of knowledge of the heart are voice and letters.

who is the epitome of phenomenal existence, and the differentia of a class is its limit or boundary from other classes. Knowledge of the heart = Divine verities. L.

[1] Wave here means human soul or reason. L.

[2] Knowledge is only communicable by language. L.

[3] Shore was before compared to speech, here to body, *i. e.* the totality of man. L.

[4] *Faiz*, emanation; *faiz-ul-kadis*, emanation of Divine grace.—De Sacy, Notices des MSS., X. 66.

[5] Compare Koran, *Sura* II. 29: "And he taught Adam the names of all things."

The soul is darting as a lightning flash,[1]
It bears these letters to the hearing ear.
Then break open the shell, take out the royal pearl,
Cast away the husk, carry off the sweet kernel.
Dictionary, etymology, syntax and accidence
Are all only the wrappings of letters.
Whoso devotes his life to these,
Has squandered his precious life on trifling.
From his nut he gets only the dry husk,
He finds no kernel unless he breaks the husk.
Nevertheless without a husk the kernel ripens not,
From external knowledge grows the sweet knowledge of faith.
O soul of my brother, hearken to my counsel!
With heart and soul strive for the knowledge of the faith.
For the 'knower' gains high place in both worlds,
Though he be humble, yet by this is he exalted.
An action which proceeds from good 'states' of heart
Is much better than this mere knowledge of the 'word.'[2]
But an action which proceeds from water and clay[3]
Equals not this knowledge, for this is the action of the heart.
See what a difference there is between body and soul;
You may take one as the east, the other as the west.
Hence learn at full how bodily actions[4]
Are related to knowledge of the word as this knowledge to 'states.'
Knowledge is not that which loves the world,
Which has the form, but is void of the reality.
Knowledge is never coupled with lust of the world,

[1] *Nafs* has here the double sense of soul and wind, blowing the pearl-oysters to the shore. L.

[2] The end of knowledge is action or practice, and practice of virtuous acts leads to the acquirement of good habits, 'states' or knowledge of heart, or ecstatic states. L.

[3] *I. e.* from the body, mere bodily acts. L.

[4] Bodily actions are to knowledge of the word or of the faith or external science, *'ilm ul yakin,* as body is to soul; and again knowledge of the word is to 'states' or knowledge of heart, *'ayn ul yakin,* as bodily actions to knowledge of the word. L.

If you desire the angel, cast out the dog.
Knowledge of faith springs from angelic virtues,
It enters not a heart with a dog's nature.
Thus runs the saying of "the Chosen,"[1]
Mark it well, for verily it is so.
When form is contained in the house,
The angels enter it not perforce.
Go, cleanse the face of the tablets of your heart,
That an angel may make his abode with you.
Gain from him the knowledge that is your heritage,
Begin to till your field for the next world's harvest.
Read the books of "The Truth"—your soul and the heavens,[2]
Be adorned with the principle[3] of all the virtues.

Rule.

ON VIRTUES AND GOOD DISPOSITIONS.

The principles of a good character are equity,
And thereafter wisdom, temperance, courage.
He who is endued with all these four
Is a sage perfect in thought and deed.[4]
His soul and heart are well informed with wisdom,
He is neither over cunning nor a fool.[5]
By temperance his appetites are subdued,

[1] Alluding to the *Hadis*, "An angel enters not a house where there are dogs or rms."

[2] Koran, *Sura* XLI. 53: "We will show them our signs in the quarters of the eavens, and in their own souls." See a passage from Kant quoted in Hamilton's etaphysics, I. 38:—"Two things there are which the oftener and the more steadstly we consider them, fill the mind with an ever-new and an ever-increasing admiraon and reverence,—the starry heaven above, and the moral law within."

[3] *I. e.*, equipoise or the mean.

[4] "The sage is he who knows things as they are (speculative wisdom), and acts he ought (practical wisdom)."—*Akhlak-i-Nasiri*, Preface.

[5] This Aristotelian doctrine of the 'mean' is found in the *Akhlak-i-Nasiri*, I. 4, d in the *Akhlak-i-Jalali*, I. 4, where also occurs the comparison with the bridge. e Esdras, ii. 7.

Intemperance and insensibility [1] alike are banished.
The courageous man is pure from abjectness and from boasting
His nature is exempt from cowardice and rashness.
Equity is as the garment of his nature,
He is void of injustice, thus his character is good.
All the virtues lie in the mean,
Which is alike removed from excess and defect.
The mean is as the '*narrow way*,' [2]
On either side yawns hell's bottomless pit.
In fineness and sharpness as a sword,
One may not turn round nor stand on it long.
Since equity has only one opposite vice,
The total number of opposite vices is seven.
Beneath each number is hidden a mystery,
For this cause has hell seven gates.[3]
Like as hell is prepared for iniquity,
Heaven is the place always appointed for equity.
Light and mercy are the recompense of equity,
Darkness and cursing the requital of iniquity.
Goodness is made manifest in equity,
Equipoise in a body is its summit of perfection.
Since a compound is as one entity,
It is remote from its parts in its nature and differentia.[4]
It becomes like to a simple essence,
And between it and simple essence there is a bond ; [5]

[1] *Khamad*, 'letting the fire out,' 'insensibility,' *anæsthesia* (Nicom. Eth., III. 10 *Akhlak-i-Nasiri*, I. part II., chapter 5.

[2] This refers to the bridge over hell. Compare couplet 382, note.

[3] Koran, *Sura* XV. 44 :—"Hell hath seven gates." So in the *Midrash*.—Rodwe *sub loco*.

[4] Lahiji says fire, water, earth, and air, the four elements of which bodies are com pounded, lose their individual qualities in the compound bodies, and equipoi (equity) is what unites them into homogeneous compounds. See Grant, Nic machæan Ethics, I. 204.

[5] In *Akhlak-i-Jalali*, I. 5, it is said :—"The connection of soul with body is b means of a perfect proportion or equipoise existing between the elementary particle wherefore the dissolution of that proportion effects the severance of that connectio

Not that bond which subsists between the compound and its parts,
(For spirit is free from the attributes of corporeity,)
But when water and clay are purified altogether,[1]
Spirit is added to them by "The Truth."[2]
When the parts, to wit, the elements attain equilibrium,
The beams of the spirit world fall upon them.
The Spirit's rays shining on the body at the time of equilibrium,
Are like the rays of the sun shining upon the earth.

Illustration.[3]

Though the sun abides in the fourth heaven,
Yet his rays are the light which rule the earth.
The elementary temperaments exist not in the sun,
The stars are not hot or cold, dry or moist.
Yet by him the elements are made warm or cold,
White, red, green, pink or yellow.
His command goes forth as that of a just prince,
One cannot say whether it is without or within the elements.
When the elements are adjusted in equipoise,
The Soul is, as it were, enamoured of their beauty,
A mystical marriage comes to pass according to the *right faith*[4]
The world is the dowry given to man by the Universal Soul.[5]
Of this marriage the issue is eloquence,

(*i. e.* death)." The same doctrine is found in Al Farabi, '*Ayún-ul-Masail*, chapter xix. See Schmölders, Documenta, p. 114, and Milton's Paradise Lost, V. 470.

[1] *I. e.* man's body. L.

[2] Koran, *Sura* XV. 29:—"We breathed into him of our spirit." Equipoise of body is what attracts this increment of spirit. L.

[3] This explains how the connection of spirit with body is not by way of a compound, but by way of *nexus*, spirit being attached *ab extra* to body. L. Compare Tauler, quoted in Vaughan, I. 62: "God pours himself out into our spirit, as the sun rays forth its natural light into the air, and fills it with sunshine, so that no eye can tell the difference between the sunshine and the air. If the union of the sun and air cannot be distinguished, how far less this divine union of the created body and uncreated spirit."

[4] Koran, *Sura* IX. 36: "This is the right faith." The marriage is between reasonable soul, *nafs-i-natika*, the 'essence of man,' and body, the 'form of man.' L.

[5] Universal Soul is the compendium of all particular souls. L.

Knowledge, language, virtue, earthly beauty.
Heavenly beauty[1] descends from the unseen world,
Descends like some licentious reveller,
Sets up its flag in the strong city of earthly beauty,
Throws into confusion all the world's array.
Now riding royally on the steed of comeliness,
Now brandishing the keen sword-blade of language.
When beheld in a person it is called beauty,
And when heard in speech eloquence.[2]
Saints, kings, durveshes, apostles,
All alike bow down and own its sway.
What is this charm in the beauty of a fair face?[3]
It is not merely earthly beauty, say what is it?[4]
That heart ravishment can come only from "The Truth,"
For there is no partner in Divine agency.[5]
How can it be lust which ravishes men's hearts?
For "The Truth" now and again appears as evil.[6]
Confess the '*working*' of "The Truth" in every place,[7]
Set not foot beyond your own limits.
Know "The Truth" in the garb of good is the true faith,
"The Truth" in the garb of evil is the work of Satan.[8]

[1] *Mulakat*, heavenly, which is the motive power of earthly beauty. Lahiji says it is a spark from the light of Unity, and is one though manifested in various theatres.

[2] "In truth there is one and the same principle, which, if prevailing in the attempered elementary particles is equipoise of temperament, if produced in musical tones is excellent and delightful intervals, if apparent in the gestures is grace, if found in language is eloquence, if produced in the human limbs is beauty, if in the qualities of the soul equity. Of this principle the Soul is enamoured and in search, whatever form it may take, whatever dress assume."—*Akhlak-i-Jalali*, I. 5. This idea comes from Plato. See Jowett's Plato, III. 138.

[3] Alluding to Koran, *Sura* XXXIII. 52:—"Though their beauty charm thee."

[4] Compare Sadi's *Diwan*:

> "I know not what sort of shrine is the brow of the fair,
> For if an atheist beholds it, he presently falls to prayer."

[5] It is Divine beauty displayed in earthly beauties which attracts all hearts. L.

[6] Evil, *batil*, vain, false, 'what is without God.'

[7] See note on couplet 673.

[8] Lahiji says legal good and evil are both manifestations of "The Truth," because

QUESTION XI.

What is that part which is greater than its whole?
What is the way to find that part?

ANSWER XI.

635 Know Absolute Being is that part which is greater than its whole,
The whole is actual being, which is the universe.[1]
Actual being bears plurality on its outside,[2]
For it contains unity only inwardly.
Every actual being is manifested through plurality,
For this is as a veil of its unity part.
Though this whole is to outward aspect many,
It is smaller in quantity than its own part.[3]
But in fine actual existence is not Necessary,
For actual existence is a vassal of Necessary Being.
640 This whole has not real absolute being,
For it is as a contingent accident of Reality.
The existence of this whole is both plural and single,
And it appears as plural through its plural aspect.

"There is no worker in creation save Allah," but yet evil comes not from God but rom 'other,' *i. e.* notbeing. See couplet 871. This resembles the view of Augustine und Aquinas, viz. that evil is a negation, a departure from God, the source and sum of all existence (Mozley, Augustinian doctrine of Predestination, 253). The Koran s in one department of its language necessitarian, and in another department it uses he language of free-will. Compare *Sura* XCI. 8. with IV. 81. At one time it ays God originates everything, evil included, at another it ascribes evil to man's vill or Satan's. (See Mozley, *ib.*, p. 36.)

[1] Lahiji says, "Absolute Being, *wajud*, by the individualization, *tashakkas*, and henomenalization, *ta'ayyun*, which occur to it, gets the name of *maujud*, actual being, und therefore *wajud* is a part of every *maujud*; for *maujud* is *wajud* plus *ta'ayyun*.—Absolute Being again is greater than its whole because it contains all *maujud*."

[2] *I.e.*, on its phenomenal side. Compare couplet 451.

[3] Because Absolute Being is the *summum genus* embracing all species of actual beings beneath it. L. The Neo Platonists and Dionysius the pseudo Arcopagite held a similar view.—Vaughan, I. 96.

Actual being is contingent, for it is a conjunction,[1]
The contingent is ever hastening of itself to not being.
In every part of this whole, as it becomes non-existent,
This whole itself is becoming non-existent on its contingent side.
The world is this whole, and in every '*twinkling of an eye*,'
It becomes non-existent and "*endures not two moments*."
Then over again another world is produced,
Every moment a new heaven and a new earth.[2]
Every moment it is a youth and an old man,
Every moment it is gathered and dispersed.
Things remain not in it two moments,
The same moment they perish, they are born again.
But this is not the great resurrection day,[3]
This is the day of works, that the '*day of faith*.'
Between this and that is a great difference, Beware!
In ignorance make not yourself entangled.
Open your eyes to see amplification and epitome,[4]
Behold hour, day, month and year.

ILLUSTRATION.

If you desire to understand this mystery,
Consider how you also have both life and death.
Of every thing in the world above or below[5]
An exemplar is set forth in your soul and body.
Like you the world is a specific person,
You are to it a soul, and it is a body to you.

[1] Conjunction, *ijtamá'i*, coalescence. A compound which contains a perishable part is dissolved and perishes when that part perishes. L.

[2] The world is changed in place, time, and quality every moment. Every moment it is clothed with fresh effluxes of Divine manifestations. L.

[3] *Tamat i kubra*, literally the great overthrow or calamity, *Sura* LXXIX. 34; also called *yaum i din*, 'day of faith,' *Sura* I. 4.

[4] The day of judgment is an amplification of the death and resurrection of phenomena occurring every moment, just as a year is of a day. L.

[5] *I. e.*, spirits and material elements. L.

Death occurs to man in three sorts ;[1]
The one every moment is that due to his nature ;[2]
Of the other two, know one is the death of his will,
The third death is that compulsory on him.
And as death and life answer to one another,
His life is of three sorts in three stages.[3]
The world has not the death of will,
For you alone of all creatures have this death.
But every moment the world is changed,
And its last state becomes like to its first.
And whatever will be seen in the world at the last day,
Will be also seen in you in your death agony.
Your body is as earth, your head as heaven,
Your senses as stars, your soul as the sun.
Your bones are as the mountains, for they are hard,
Your hair as plants, and your limbs as trees.
On the day of death your body with contrition
Will '*tremble*' like the earth on the day of doom.[4]
Brain will be confounded and soul darkened,
Your senses will become dim like the stars,[5]
Your pores will run with sweat like the rivers,
You will be drowned therein as a helpless log.
In your death agony, O wretched man !
Your bones will become "*soft as dyed wool,*"[6]
Leg will be twisted with leg,[7]

[1] Lahiji says :—The first death is that which every existing thing dies, and is ery moment born again ; the second the ascetic death to the world, according to e text, "Die before you die ;" and the third the separation of soul and body. The st death seems to be the Heracleitean doctrine of the flux of all things *(rei*). Heracleitus is quoted in a passage of Jelál-ud-dín Rúmi, given in Lumsden's ersian Grammar, II. 323.

[2] *I. e.*, necessitated by the contingent phenomenal element in him. L.

[3] One in this world, one in the world to come, another in hades. L.

[4] Koran, *Sura* XCIX. 1 : "The earth shall tremble with her trembling."

[5] Koran, *Sura* LXXXI. 2.

[6] Koran, *Sura* CI. 4.

[7] Koran, *Sura* LXXV. 29.

Every friend will be separated from his fellow.[1]
And when spirit is wholly separated from body,
Your land will be "*a level plain, without hills or valleys*."[2]
In like manner will be the state of the world,
Which you behold in yourself at that hour.
Permanence belongs to "The Truth," all else is fleeting,
Its whole fabric is set forth in the "*seven chapters*."[3]
Which say "*all that is on earth is transitory*,"[4]
And show forth "*the new creation*."[5]
Again the constant annihilation and renovation of the tw
worlds
Are like the creation and resurrection of the sons of Adam.
Continually is creation born again in a new creation,
Though the duration of its life seems long.[6]
Continually the overflowing bounty of "The Truth"
Is being revealed in His continual "*working*."[7]
On this side the world is renewed and perfected,
On that side it is every moment annihilated.[8]
But when the fashion of this world passes away,
All will be everlasting in the world to come.
For every object which you see of necessity
Contains two worlds, form and reality.
The "union" of the first is true separation,
The other is what endures for ever in Allah.[9]
Permanence is a name proper to Necessary Being,
But yet the place where Being dwells is also permanent,[10]

[1] Koran, *Sura* LXX: "A friend shall not ask of a friend."
[2] Koran, *Sura* XX. 105.
[3] See note on couplet 207.
[4] Koran, *Sura* LV. 26.
[5] Koran, *Sura* L. 14. and XXIX. 17. Compare Rev. xxi. 1. 5.
[6] Owing to the rapidity of the phenomenal effluxes from Being, the phenomenal lif of the creature world seems continuous. L.
[7] "He is working every day."—Koran, *Sura* LV. 29. See John v. 17.
[8] This side=God; that side the phenomenal contingent. L.
[9] Koran, *Sura* XVI. 98.
[10] *I. e.*, so long as Being lodges in it. L.

When the manifestors are suitable to what is manifested,
In this world is seen the world to come.[1]
Whatsoever exists in potentiality in this "house,"
Will come into actuality in the world to come.[2]

Rule.[3]

Whatever action once proceeds from you,
If you repeat it several times, you become master of it.
Every time you repeat it, be it gain or loss,
One of these two becomes implanted in your soul.
By habit dispositions become habitual,
By length of time fruits gain their savour.
By habitual practice men learn their trades,
By habit they learn to collect their thoughts.
All man's ingrained actions and sayings
Will be made manifest at the last day.[4]
When you are stripped of the garment of this body,[5]
All your vices and virtues will at once be shown.
A body you will have, but one free from stain,[6]
In it will be reflected forms as in pure water.
All secrets will be revealed in that place,
Read the text "*All secrets shall be searched out.*"[7]

[1] When the contingent mirrors of Divine effluxes are polished and fit to reflect the "Manifested," then the invisible is seen in the visible world. L.

[2] Here is another reproduction of the Aristotelian doctrines of *Dynamis* and *Energeia*, and of habits.

[3] This Rule explains how mental qualities will in the world to come be embodied in forms or bodies suitable to evidence and manifest them properly. When Divine names are manifested in suitable mirrors these mirrors are everlasting. L.

[4] Dispositions, freed from the stain of the phenomenal, will then be reflected in perfect mirrors. L.

[5] Compare Plato, *Gorgias*: "And, in a word, whatever was the habit of the body during life would be distinguishable after death. . . . . When the man is stripped of his body, all the natural or acquired affections of the soul are laid open to view."—Jowett's Plato, III. 123. See Rev. xxii. 11.

[6] See 1 Cor. xv. 44. In the *Sharh makhtasar* it is said, soul cannot be without a body, and after death it has an "acquired body," a shadowy figure.

[7] Koran, *Sura* LXXXVI. 9.

Again, suitably to that special world
Your dispositions will be embodied and personified.
Just as in this world from the potentialities of elements
The three kingdoms of nature are produced.[1]
So all your dispositions in the world of spirits
Will be made manifest now as lights, now as fires.[2]
Phenomenal limitations will be removed from Being,
Nor height nor depth will remain in sight.[3]
The death of the body will abide not in the '*house of life*,'[4]
External form and soul will appear as one stainless entity.
Your head, foot and eye will become as a heart,
Pure from the stain of earthly form.
Then the light of "The Truth" will illuminate you,
You will behold face to face "The Truth" Most High.
I know not what intoxication will possess you,
You will scatter in confusion the two worlds.
Consider what means "*their Lord gives them to drink*,"[5]
And what is "*pure wine*"! It is purification from self.
What a draught, what lusciousness, what sweetness!
What bliss, what ecstasy, what intoxication!
O happy moment when we shall quit our "selves"!
When we shall be most rich in utterest poverty![6]
Without faith or reason, or piety or perception,
Bowed down in the dust, drunken and beside ourselves!

[1] Lahiji, quoting from the *Hakk ul Yakin*, says potentialities of origin, *mubd* come into actuality in the present life, *m'aash*; *e.g.* from the potentialities of t elements come forth minerals, animals and men; and so the inner potentialities acquir by men in this world, *m'aash*, are developed by habit into actuality and eviden in the next world, *mu'ad*, and there find fit mirrors or forms to represent them.

[2] *I.e.* heaven and hell.

[3] Rom. viii. 39.

[4] Koran, *Sura* XXIX. 64: "Verily the future house is life indeed." Lahiji sa that 'knowers' attain this stage in the present life.

[5] "And their Lord shall give them to drink of a most pure wine."—Koran, *Su* LXXVI. 21.

[6] Poor, *i.e.* by effacing self, and rich by union with "The Truth." L.

Of what account then will be paradise and houris ?[1]
For no stranger finds entrance to that secret chamber.
When I have seen this vision, and drunk of this cup,
I know not what will come to pass thereafter.
Nay, after all intoxication comes headache,[2]
This thought again drowns my soul in blood.

QUESTION XII.

How are eternal and temporal separate,[3]
That one is the world, and the other God ?

ANSWER XII.

Eternal and temporal are not separate from one another.
For in that Being this non-existent has its being.
The first is all in all, the other is like the 'Anka,[4]
Save "The Truth" no names have things answering to them.
Not being to become existent—this is impossible,
But real Being in point of existence is imperishable.
Neither does this become that, nor that this.
All difficulties are now plain before you ;
The whole world is merely an imaginary thing,
It is like one point whirled round in a circle.
Go ! whirl round a single spark of fire,
And from its quick motion you will see a circle.

[1] These all partake of the phenomenal, and are external to real Unity and Unification, *tauhid*. Lahiji cites :

"While heaven and hell stand in your way,
How is your soul cognizant of this mystery ?"

See couplet 338.

[2] States of ecstasy in this life are only temporary, and are followed by the reappearance of veils and phenomena. L.

[3] *Kadm.* The 'ancient of days,' the self-existent, the Being who is first and not preceded by another. *Das Ur*, usually opposed to *'adm*. Tholuck, Ssufismus, 194.

[4] A fabulous bird said to be "known by name, but unknown in the body." Like it, the temporal is an empty name. L.

Though one be counted again and again,[1]
Yet surely one becomes not many by this counting.
Cast away the saying "*What is other than Allah*"
By your own reason separate that from this.
How can you doubt that this is a dream ?[2]
For duality by the side of unity is a pure delusion.
Not being is single like being,
All plurality proceeds from attribution.[3]
The manifestation of differences and plurality of things
Proceed from the chameleon contingent.[4]
Since the Being in all of them is One,[5]
They all bear witness to the unity of "The Truth."

QUESTION XIII.

What means the mystic by those expressions of his[6]
What does he indicate by "eye" and "lip ?"
What seeks he by "cheek," "curl," "down," and "mole ?"
He, to wit, who is in "stations" and "states ?"[7]

ANSWER XIII.

Whatsoever is seen in this visible world,

[1] Compare the saying of Mansur Hallaj: "The counting of Unity makes th numbers of Unity."

[2] *I.e.* this temporal.

[3] *I.e.* attribution of Being in its various aspects and 'names' to Not Being. L.

[4] Chameleon contingent means *'ayan i sabita*. See note on couplet 273.

[5] Each reflects one special name according to its capacity. L. See couplet 278.

[6] Mystic, *mard i ma'niy*. He who turns his face from the world of forms to that o verity, and holds intuitive certainty. L. *Ma'niy*, interior rei conditio. Freytag.

[7] See *Istilahat us Sufiah*, p. 35: "*Hal*, 'state,' is that which occurs to the hear spontaneously and without effort, like grief or fear, or expansion or cheerfulness, o desire or joy, and which ceases as soon as the natural dispositions of the soul manifes themselves, without being followed by similar states, for if a state becomes predo minant, it is called *mukam*, 'station.'" This definition is evidently derived fron Aristotle's account of *energeia* and *hexis*. . "And, in a word, from like energies aris habits."—Nicom. Eth. II. 1, 7. The Sufis applied the words to ecstatic states. Se couplet 585.

Is as a reflection from the sun of that world.
The world is as curl, down, mole and brow,
For everything in its own place is beautiful.
The epiphany is now in beauty, now in majesty,[1]
Cheek and curl are the similitudes of those verities.
The attributes of "The Truth" are mercy and vengeance,
Cheek and curl of fair ones are types of these two.
When these words are heard by the sensual ear,
At first they denote objects of sense.
The spiritual world is infinite,
How can finite words attain to it?[2]
How can the mysteries beheld in ecstatic vision
Be interpreted by spoken words?
When mystics treat of these mysteries,
They interpret them by types.
For objects of sense are as shadows of that world,[3]
And this world is as an infant, and that as the nurse,
I believe that these words were at first assigned
To those mysteries in their original usage.
They were afterwards assigned to objects of sense by usage of the vulgar
(For what know the vulgar of these mysteries?)
And when reason turned its glance on the world,
It transferred some words from that place.[4]
The wise man has regard to analogy,
When he turns his mind to words and mysteries.
Although perfect analogies are unattainable,
Nevertheless continue steadfast in seeking them.

[1] Koran, *Sura* LV. 27: "But the face of thy Lord shall endure, clothed with auty and (terrible) majesty," *i.e. jamal* and *jalal.* See note on couplet 633.

[2] Compare couplet 54.

[3] See Milton's Paradise Lost, V. 574:

"What if earth
Be but the shadow of heaven, and things therein
Each to other like, more than on earth is thought?"

[4] *I.e.* to sensible objects from spiritual. L.

In this matter none can judge you,
For there is no leader of the sect here save "The Truth."[1]
Yet so long as you retain yourself, Beware! Beware!
And observe the expressions used in the law.
The license of mystics is in three "states,"[2]
Annihilation, intoxication, and the fever of love.
All who experience these three "states"
Know the use of these words and their meanings.
But if you experience not these "states"
Be not an ignorant infidel blindly repeating them.[3]
These mystic "states" are not mere illusions,
All men reach not the mysteries of the mystic path.
O friend, vain babbling proceeds not from men of truth,
To know these states requires either revelation or faith.[4]
I have explained the usage of words and their meanings
To you in brief, and if you attend you will understand.
In applying them look to their final intent,
And regard all the attributes of each.
Use them in comparisons in manner proper thereto,
Carefully abstain from applying them otherwise.
Now that this rule is well established,
I will show you more of these types.

Indication
of the eye and the lip.

See what proceeds from the eye and the lip,

[1] Because these mysteries are apprehended only in ecstatic states. L. Compare 1 Cor. ii. 15: "He that is spiritual judgeth all things, yet he himself is judged of no man."

[2] *I. e.*, when mystics are beside themselves, and powerless to control their expressions. L. Compare Jeremy Taylor: "When they suffer transportations beyond the burden and support of reason, they suffer they know not what, and call it what they please."

[3] Unless a man personally experience ecstatic states his use of their types is mere *taklid* (L.), *i. e.* cant, blindly copying or repeating.

[4] If you cannot experience them you must take them in trust. L.

Consider their attributes in this place.[1]
From His eye proceed languishing and intoxication,
From His ruby lip[2] the essence of being.[3]
Because of His eye all hearts are burning,
His ruby lip is healing to the sick heart.
Because of His eye hearts are drunken and aching,
By His ruby lip all souls are clothed.[4]
Though the world is not regarded by His eye,
His lip ever and anon shows compassion.
Sometimes with humanity He charms our hearts,
Sometimes He grants help to the helpless.
By smiles He gives life to man's water and clay,
By a breath He kindles the heaven into a flame.[5]
Every glance of His eye is a snare baited with corn,
Every corner thereof is a wine shop.
With a frown He lays waste the creature world,
With one kiss He restores it again every moment.
Because of His eye our blood is ever boiling,
Because of His lip our souls are ever beside themselves.
By a frown of His eye He plunders the heart,
By a smile on His lips He cheers the soul.
When you ask of His eye and lip an embrace,[6]
One says "nay," and the other "yea."
By a frown He finishes the affair of the world,
By a kiss He ever and anon revives the soul.

[1] *I. e.*, in the world of mystery. Eye signifies frowns and coquetry holding aloof from its slave, lip mercy and kindness granting union. L.

[2] See Hafiz, Ode 305 (Brockhause):

> "Since first Hafiz learned to tell the story of Thy ruby lip,
> From his pen the eternal fount of life is flowing evermore."

[3] Koran, *Sura* XV. 29: "We breathed into him of our spirit," which the Sufis interpret as the constant efflux of Being by which all things subsist,—the *khila't* of Being thrown over the nakedness of Not being. L. See couplet 645.

[4] Literally, 'veiled.' Compare Psalm xxxii. 1: "Whose sin is covered."

[5] *I. e.*, of jealousy, because the Divine 'deposit' was entrusted to man. L. See note on couplet 264.

[6] *I. e.*, union with the Absolute. L.

One frown from Him and we yield up our lives,
One kiss from Him and we rise again.
As the "*twinkling of an eye*"[1] comes the last day,
By a breath the spirit of Adam was created.
When the world reflects on His eye and His lip,
It gives itself up to the worship of wine.[2]
All existence is not regarded by His eyes,
They regard it only as the illusion of a dream.
Man's existence is but intoxication or a sleep,
What relation does the dust bear to the Lord of Lords?
Reason draws a hundred perplexities from this
That He said "*thou mightest be formed after mine eye.*"[3]

Indication

of the curl.[4]

The story of the curl of The Beloved is very long,
What is it meet to tell of this seeing it is a mystery?
Ask not of me the story of that knotted curl,
It is a chain leading mad lovers captive.
Last night I spoke straightforwardly of that stately form,[5]
But the tip of the curl replied, "Conceal it."
Thence crookedness prevailed over straightness,
And the enquirer's path was twisted awry.
By that curl all hearts are enchained,[6]
By that curl all souls are borne to and fro.

[1] Koran, *Sura* LIV. 50. See 1 Cor. xv. 52.

[2] The Eternal Cupbearer pours the wine of Being into the cup of Not being, and hence fills it with the intoxication and illusion of phenomenal being. L.

[3] Koran, *Sura* XX. 40: "I bestowed my love upon thee, that thou mightest be fashioned after mine eye."

[4] Curl means plurality veiling the face of Unity from its lovers. L.

[5] *I. e.*, Unity. L.

[6] *I. e.*, from beholding Unity. See Hafiz (Brockhaus), Ode 338:

"From the meshes of thy tresses there are none who can get free,
Thou dost slay thy wretched lovers with no fear of penalty."

A hundred thousand hearts are bound on every side,
No heart escapes from the yoke thereof.
If He shakes aside those black curls of His
No single infidel is left in the world.
If He leaves them continually in their place,
There remains not in the world one faithful soul.
That spider's web of His is spread as a net to ensnare,
In wantonness He puts it aside from off His face.[1]
If His curls were shorn, what harm were it?
If night were destroyed, would not day be increased?
As He plunders the caravan of reason,
With His own hands He binds it with knots.[2]
That curl is never at rest for a moment,
Now it brings morning and now evening.
With His face and His curl He makes day and night,
Sporting with them in marvellous fashion.[3]
The clay of Adam became leavened at the moment
When it caught the perfume of that amber scented curl.[4]
My heart holds of that curl an ensample,[5]
So that it too cannot rest for a moment.
Therefore every moment must I begin my work afresh,[6]
And pluck my heart out of my bosom.
Therefore is my heart troubled by that curl,
Because it veils my burning heart from His face.

[1] See Hafiz, Ode 10:

"My bosom's fowl spread out his net, and caught peace for his prey,
Then thou didst loose that net thy hair, and peace straight flew away."

[2] Reason cannot transcend plurality. L.

[3] Compare the Vulgate: "Ludens in orbe terrarum." By veiling and unveiling His face, He makes light and darkness, faith and infidelity, &c. L.

[4] Adam obtained the 'deposit,'—the faculty of displaying all the Divine attributes,—when the *khila't* of plurality was conferred on him. L.

[5] Heart is the epitome of man, who is the epitome of the world of phenomena. Hence it contains all the opposite qualities, light and dark, good and evil, &c. L.

[6] *I. e.*, plurality obscures Unity afresh. L.

Indication

OF THE CHEEK AND THE DOWN.[1]

The cheek in this place is the theatre of Divine beauty,
And the down signifies the vestibule of Almightiness.
His cheek scores a line through beauty,
Saying "without me is no comeliness of face."[2]
The down is a verdant growth in the spirit world
Therefore is it named the "*mansion of life.*"[3]
With the blackness of His curl turn day into night,
In His down seek the well-spring of life.
Like Khizr the prophet in a "*hidden place*"[4]
Like His down, quaff the water of life.[5]
If you see His face and His down, of a surety
You will know plurality and unity every whit.[6]
From the curl you learn the affair of this world,
In the down you read at large the "*the hidden secret.*"
If one sees the down on His face,
Yet my heart sees His face in that down.[7]
His cheek is as the "*seven verses,*"[8]
Every letter whereof is an ocean of mysteries.
Hidden beneath each hair on that cheek
Are a thousand oceans of mysteries from the unseen world.

[1] The cheek means the Divine essence in respect of the manifestation of all its names and qualities. The down is the world of pure spirits, which is nearest to Divinity. L. See couplet 120.

[2] His manifested beauty sums up and surpasses all beauty. L.

[3] Koran, *Sura* XXIX. 64: "Truly the future mansion is life indeed."

[4] See note on couplet 124.

[5] Passing from land of darkness, *i. e.* the veil of plurality, quaff the water of life (unity), in the verdant mead, or oasis or down (the spirit world). L.

[6] The down—the spirit world—is the first plural emanation which veils the face of unity. L. Curl, the sensible world.

[7] One sees the phenomenal world, and infers from it "The Truth;" another sees "The Truth" first in all that he sees. See couplet 85. L.

[8] *I.e. Fatiha,* which contains the whole essence of the Koran, as the cheek is the manifestation of the seven names of God. L.

790 See the heart is the "throne of God on the water,"[1]
The down on the cheek is the adornment of souls.

INDICATION

OF THE MOLE.[2]

On that cheek the point of His mole is single,
It is a centre which is the basis of the circling circumference.
From that centre is drawn the circle of the two worlds,
From that centre Adam's heart and soul.
Because of that mole the heart is bleeding sore,
For it is a reflection of the point of the black mole,[3]
Like His mole the state of the heart is black blood,
For there is no way of escape from that station.
795 Plurality finds not entrance into Unity,
There are no two points in the root of Unity.[4]
I know not if His mole is the reflection of my heart,
Or my heart the reflection of the mole on that fair face.
If my heart springs from the reflection of His mole,
Or if the reflection of my heart is seen in that place.[5]
If my heart is in His face, or that mole in my heart,
This dark secret is hidden from me.
If this heart of mine be the reflection of that mole,
Why are its states so various?[6]

[1] Alluding to the *Hadis*: "The heart of the believer is the throne of God," and the text, "His throne was set on the water."—Koran, *Sura* XI. 9. The heart is the down or oasis (spirit world) sprouting on the face like water. L.

[2] Mole means the point of Unity—the 'hidden Ipseity,' single in itself, but embracing all phenomena. L.

[3] See note on couplet 151. Both are sources of life and existence. L.

[4] Hence Unity and heart must be one. Which is the original, and which the reflection? L.

[5] *I.e.* His face. L.

[6] The point of Unity is fixed and stable, but the heart is disquieted by constant change of emotions, brightened by Divine epiphanies and darkened by the veil of plurality, now in the spiritual mosque, now in the formal synagogue, now sunk in the hell of carnal affections, now raised to the heaven of spiritual emotions. L.

Sometimes it is sick like His intoxicating eye,
Sometimes fluttering like His curl.
Sometimes gleaming as a moon like that face,
Sometimes dark like that black mole.
Sometimes it is a mosque, sometimes a synagogue,
Sometimes a hell, sometimes a heaven.
Sometimes exalted above the seventh heaven,
Sometimes sunken below 'this mound' of earth.
After devotion and asceticism it becomes again
Addicted to wine, lamp and beauty.

QUESTION XIV.

What meaning attaches to wine, torch, and beauty?
What is assumed in being a haunter of taverns?[1]

ANSWER XIV.

Wine, torch, and beauty are epiphanies of Verity,
For it is that which is revealed under all forms soever.
Wine and torch are the transport and light of the 'knower,'
Behold 'The Beauty' for it is hidden from none.[2]
Here wine is the lamp-shade, torch the lamp,
And Beauty the beam of the light of spirits.
By Beauty were kindled sparks in the heart of Moses,
His wine was the fire, and his torch the burning bush.[3]
Wine and torch are the soul of that flashing light,
Beauty signifies that '*greatest of signs.*'[4]

[1] Wine is the rapture making the Sufi beside himself at the apparition or emanations of The Beloved; torch, the light kindled in his heart by the same apparition and Beauty, The Truth itself manifested and present. L.

[2] When the veil of self is removed. L.

[3] See notes on couplets 292 and 192.

[4] This refers to Muhammad, who beheld a higher revelation than Moses when he ascended by night to heaven and witnessed God as a light. "He saw the greatest of the signs of his Lord."—Koran, *Sura* LIII. 18.

Wine, torch, and beauty, all are present,
Neglect not to embrace that Beauty.
Quaff the wine of dying to self, and for a season
Peradventure you will be freed from the dominion of self.
Drink wine that it may set you free from yourself,
And may conduct the being of the drop to the ocean.[1]
Drink wine, for its cup is the face of "The Friend,"
The cup is His eye drunken and flown with wine.
Seek wine without cup or goblet,
Wine is wine-drinker, cupbearer is winecup.[2]
Drink wine from the cup of "*the face that endures*,"[3]
The text "*their Lord gave them to drink*" is its cupbearer.[4]
Pure wine is that which gives you purification
From the stain of existence at the time of intoxication.
Drink wine and rid yourself of coldness of heart,
For a drunkard is better than the self-righteous.
The man who dwells far from the portals of "The Truth,"
For him the veil of darkness is better than the veil of light.[5]
Thus Adam found a hundred blessings from darkness,[6]
And Iblis was eternally cursed through the light.
Though the mirror of the heart be polished,[7]

[1] *I. e.*, the drop freed from its phenomenal limitation, 'dropness.' L.

[2] *I. e.*, the wine of ecstatic absorption in Unity annuls all phenomenal plurality, akes us 'beside ourselves,' and reduces all to Unity. L.

[3] Koran, *Sura* LV. 26.

[4] Koran, *Sura* LXXVI. 21.

[5] 'Veil of darkness' means dwelling in iniquity, 'veil of light' the practice of ood works. He who is veiled by the former knows his own baseness, but he who is eiled by the latter knows it not, being clouded by his own conceit of self-righteousness. oran, *Sura* XVIII. 103: "Shall we tell you who are they that have lost their bour most, whose aim in this life hath been mistaken? they who think that what ey do is right." L. Compare:

"The fool simple is he who knows that he knows not,
The fool complex he who knows not that he knows not."

[6] Adam confessed his sin, saying, "O Lord, we have darkened our souls."—Koran, *ura* VII. 22.—Satan's pride of origin from fire led to his fall. "Me thou hast eated of fire." *Sura* XXXVIII. 77. Compare Heb. i. 7.

[7] *I. e.* by good works. L.

What profit is it when only self is seen on its face.
When a ray from His face falls upon the wine,
Many forms are seen on it as it were bubbles.[1]
World and spirit world are seen on it as bubbles,
Its bubbles are to the saints as veils.
Universal Reason is dazed and beside itself at this,
Universal Soul is reduced to slavery.[2]
The whole universe is as His winehouse,
The heart of every atom as His winecup.[3]
Reason is drunken, angels drunken, soul drunken,
Air drunken, earth drunken, heaven drunken.
The heavens giddy with this wine are reeling to and fro,
Desiring in their heart to smell its perfume.
The angels drinking it pure from pure vessels,
Pour the dregs of their draught upon this world.[4]
The elements becoming light-headed from that draught
Fall now into the fire, now into the water.
From the scent of its dregs which fell on the earth,
Man ascends up till he reaches heaven.
From its reflection the withered body becomes a living soul,[5]
From its heat the frozen soul is warmed to life and motion.
The creature world is ever dizzy therewith,
From house and home ever wandering astray.
One from the scent of its dregs becomes a philosopher,[6]
One from seeing the colour of the pure wine a traditionist.[7]
One from half a draught becomes righteous,

[1] Phenomena are as bubbles on the sea of Being. L.

[2] The wine of Divine love and ecstasy intoxicates all phenomena from the fir emanation downwards. L.

[3] The existence of every atom proceeds from the wine of Divine love. All a vessels holding Being according to their various capacities. L.

[4] The spirit world was first created, and thus quaffs the wine of Divine emanatio nearer to its source. The world is a later emanation. L.

[5] Aspiring or moving towards its source. L.

[6] These are the various grades which men attain in proportion to their capacity t receive the pure wine. L.

[7] Pure, because traditionists repeat the sayings of the prophets. L.

One from quaffing a cupful becomes a lover.
Yet another swallows at one draught
Cup, winehouse, cupbearer and wine drinker.
He swallows them all, yet his mouth remains open.
Well done, O ocean heart, O mighty wine bibber! [1]
He drinks up existence at one draught,
And obtains release from affirmations and negations.
Freed from dry devotions and empty rites,
He grasps the skirt of the ancient of the winehouse. [2]

INDICATION

OF TAVERN-HAUNTERS. [3]

To be a haunter of taverns is to be freed from self,
Self-regard is paganism, even if it be in righteousness. [4]
They have brought you news from the tavern
That unification is shaking off relations. [5]
The tavern is of the world that has no similitude,
It is the place of lovers that reck not.
The tavern is the nest of the bird of the soul,
The tavern is the sanctuary that has no place.
The tavern-haunter is desolate in a desolate place,
In his desert the world is as a mirage. [6]
This desert has no end or limit,
No man has seen its beginning or its end.
Though you wander about in it for a hundred years,
You will find there neither yourself, nor 'other.'
They that dwell therein are headless and footless,
They are neither faithful nor infidels.

See note on couplet 701.
I.e., the *Pir-i-kamil*, or Director of the Sufi pilgrim. L.
Tavern signifies Unity.
See note on couplet 819.
Compare couplet 640.
I.e., an unreal phenomenon in the expanse of Being. In this expanse all 'other' sent. L. *Kharábát* means "desert" as well as "tavern."

The wine of alienation from self has got into their heads,
They have renounced alike evil and good.
Each has drunk wine without lips or palate,
Each has cast away thought of name and fame,
Talk of marvels, of visions, and 'states,'
Dreams of secret chambers, of lights, of signs.[1]
All through the smell of these dregs have they cast away,
Through tasting this self-annihilator they are lying drunken.
Pilgrim's staff, and cruse, and rosary, and dentifrice,
All have they given as ransom for these dregs.
Falling and rising again in the midst of water and clay,[2]
Shedding blood from their eyes for tears.
Now raised by intoxication to the world of bliss,
Exalting their necks as racers.
Now with blackened faces beholding the wall,
Now with reddened faces impaled on the stake.[3]
Now in the mystic dance of joy in The Beloved,
Losing head and foot like the revolving heavens.
In every strain which they hear from the minstrel
Comes to them rapture from the unseen world.
The mystic song is not those mere words and sound,
For in every note thereof lies a precious mystery.
Putting from off their head their tenfold cloak,[4]
Being abstracted from every colour and smell;
And washing off in that pure well racked wine,
All colour, black and green and blue.
Drinking one cup of that pure wine,
And thence becoming "Sufis" cleansed from qualities;
Sweeping the dust of dung-heaps from off their souls,

[1] All these are experienced in the journey up to Unity, but are now left behind. L. See the passage from Ghazali in note on couplet 411.

[2] *I. e.*, now in the delight of 'union,' now in the aching void of separation. L.

[3] This refers to the execution of Mansur Hallaj. Now blackened by separation from the light by the wall of phenomena, now with faces reddened by the intoxicating wine of Union. L.

[4] *I. e.*, the senses external and internal. See note to couplet 124.

Telling not a hundredth part of what they see,
Grasping the skirts of drunkards flown with wine,
Wearied of teachership and discipleship.[1]
What are devotion and piety? What hypocrisy are these?
What are teachership and discipleship? What bonds are these?[2]
If your face be still set on great and small,[3]
Idols, girdles and Christianity are meet for you.[4]

QUESTION XV.

Idols, girdles and Christianity in this discourse
Are all infidelity; if not, say what they are.

ANSWER XV.

Here idol is the evidence of love and unity,
Girdle is the binding of the bond of obedience.
Since infidelity and faith are both based on Being,
Idol-worship is essentially Unification.[5]
Since all things are the manifestors of Being,
One amongst them must be an idol.
Consider well, O wise man,
An idol as regards its real being is not vain.[6]

[1] "The secrets hid behind the veil from publicans enquire,
Great devotees of high degree that knowledge ne'er attain."
Hafiz, Ode 4.

[2] *I. e.*, duality exists no more for the 'united' Sufi. L.

[3] *I. e.*, seeing distinctions where all are one. L.

[4] As a means of training you to see true Unity. L.

[5] For if 'other' exists 'unification' is impossible. 'Other' involves ***shirk***, giving rtners to God, Manichæanism. L. Compare Hafiz (Brockhaus), Ode 79:
"Between the love of the cloister and that of the tavern there is no difference,
For wherever love is, there is the light of the face of the Beloved.
Wherever the pious works of the Moslem hermitage display their beauty,
There are the bells of the Christian convent and the name of the Cross."

[6] See note on couplet 236.

Know that God Most High created it,
And whatever comes from the Good is good.
Being is purely good in whatever it be,
If it also contains evil, that proceeds from 'other.'[1]
If the Musulman but knew what is faith,
He would see that faith is idol-worship.
If the polytheist only knew what idols are,
How would he be wrong in his religion?
He sees in idols naught but the visible creature,[2]
And that is the reason that he is legally a heathen.
You also, if you see not "The Truth" hid in the idols,
In the eye of the law are not a Musulman.
By telling beads and saying prayers and reading the Koran
The heathen becomes not a Musulman.
That man is disgusted with superficial faith,
To whom the true infidelity has once been revealed.
Within every body is hidden a soul,
And within infidelity is hidden true faith.
Infidelity is ever giving praise to "The Truth;"
The text, "*All things praise God,*" proves it. Who can gair
say it?[3]
What am I saying? I have gone astray from the road?[4]
"*Leave them, and after all that is revealed, say, God,*"[5]
Who adorned the face of the idol with such beauty?
Who became an idol-worshipper, unless "The Truth" willed it
It is He that made, He that said, He that is,[6]
Made good, said good, is good.
See but One, say One, know but One,

[1] *I.e.* not being and plurality. L. See couplet 633.

[2] *I. e.* the phenomenal. L.

[3] See note on couplet 440.

[4] *I. e.* far from the road of the external positive law, but yet leave gainsayers a say of all it is God. L.

[5] "Say God (has sent down the Koran), and then leave them to amuse themselv with their vain discourses."—Koran, *Sura* VI. 91.

[6] Said, *i. e.* be an idol-worshipper. L.

In this are summed up the roots and branches of faith.
It is not I who declare this; hear it from the Koran,
"*There is no distinction in the creatures of the Merciful.*"[1]

INDICATION
OF THE GIRDLE.

The knotted girdle is the emblem of obedience.
I have looked and seen the origin of every thing,
For the wise man finds no trustworthy information
As to anything except in its original usage.[2]
Gird your loins, like a valiant man, with manliness,
Join the band who "*fulfil my covenant.*"[3]
With the horse of knowledge and the bat of obedience
Bear off from the field the ball of good fortune.
For this duty did God create you,
Albeit He created many creatures besides you.[4]
Knowledge is as a father, practice a mother
Of mystic states which are "*a joy of the eyes.*"[5]
Doubtless, there is no mortal man but has a father,[6]
There was never but one Messiah in the world.[7]
Cast aside vain tales, and mystic states and visions,
Dreams of lights, and marvels of miracles.[8]
Your miracles are comprised in "Truth" worship,[9]

[1] Koran, *Sura* LXVII. 3.

[2] See couplet 728.

[3] Koran, *Sura* II. 38: "O children of Israel, fulfil your covenant with me," *i.e.* bedience. See couplet 419.

[4] Koran, *Sura* LI. 56: "I have not created Jins and men save to serve and ey me."

[5] "No soul knoweth the joy of the eyes which is secretly prepared for them as a ward for that which they have wrought."—Koran, *Sura* XXXII. 18. See Cor. ii. 9.

[6] Knowledge, the father, is necessary, as well as obedience or practice, the mother, bring men to the good fortune of Union. L.

[7] See Koran, *Sura* III. 42.

[8] Compare couplet 849 and note.

[9] Miracles, *karamat*, also mighty works, honour, as in couplet 554.

All besides is pride, vain glory and illusion of existence.
In this path whatever is not of poverty of spirit
Is but being puffed up and seeking our own glory.[1]
By cursed Iblis, who witnesses not verity,
Are wrought thousands of miracles.
Now he approaches from the wall, now from the roof,
Now he dwells in your heart, now in your body.
He knows all the hidden counsels of your heart,
He works in you unbelief, and transgression and sin.
Iblis is the Imám, and you his followers,[2]
But how can you rival him in his miracles?
If your miracles are wrought only in self-ostentation,
You are a Pharaoh, to wit, one arrogating divinity.
But he who has fellowship with "The Truth"
Is never one who vaunts himself.
All your regard is set on creatures; Beware
That you fall not into captivity of this disease.[3]
If you consort with the base, you become an animal;
Nay, not an animal, but at once a stone.[4]
Flee from connection with the base,
Lest you fall headlong from your natural rank.
You have wasted your precious life in trifling,
You think not of what use is such a life as yours.
They call it peace when it is confusion,
They take an ass for their guide—see his beard![5]
The leadership having now devolved on fools,
All men have fallen on evil days.

[1] Miracles, if done to be seen of men, are a cause of egoism. L.

[2] Because you work miracles for self-ostentation. L.

[3] *I. e.* the wish to be thought a mighty worker of miracles. You seek the appr bation of the base, and, by consorting with them, sink to their level. L.

[4] *Naskh* transmigration of the soul into men, *maskh* into animals, *raskh* into pla and into minerals, *faskh* into all. L. See Schmölders (Documenta, p. 123).

[5] *I. e.* the mark of the popular Shaikh. L. This passage would seem to ha been written under the influence of personal animosity against some particu popular teacher, but Lahiji treats it as of only general application.

See the one-eyed *Dajjal,*[1] in what way
He is sent into the world as an ensample.
See this ensample, O man of sense!
Know him for the ass whose name is *Jassás.*
See all these asses in the toils of that ass,
Being the forerunners in ignorance of that ass.
When our lord told the story of the latter days,
In several places he signified this matter.
See now how there are blind and gluttons,
All knowledge of the faith has departed to heaven.
There remain not in the midst courtesy and modesty,
None have shame for their ignorance.
The whole condition of the world is upset;
If you are wise, see in what state it is.
One who is accursed and banned and hated
Is now Shaikh of the age, because his father was good.
Yet that wicked son was slain by Khizr,[2]
Because his father and grandfather were good.
O ass, now you have chosen for your Shaikh
An ass who is more ass-like than yourselves.
For as much as "*he knows not cat from mouse,*"[3]
How will your secret be purified through him?
If the son shows a trace of his father,
What shall I say? Verily he is light upon light.
If the son be of good judgment and fortune,
He is as fruit, the cream and perfection of the tree.
But how can he be Shaikh of the faith,
Who knows not good from evil, evil from good?
Discipleship is learning the knowledge of the faith,

[1] *Dajjal,* Antichrist, and *Jassás,* the spy, a mighty beast sixty cubits high, will appear as precursors of the last day.—Sale's Koran, Prelim. Discourse, p. 57, and *Sura* XXVII. 83, 84. 1 John ii. 18. 1 Tim. iv. 1.

[2] See Koran, *Sura* XVIII. 61. Khizr slew him because he feared that his parents would suffer for their son's perverseness.

[3] Or 'calling cattle, from driving them away,' or 'good from evil.'

Kindling with light the lamp of the heart.
Did ever one learn knowledge from the dead?
Was ever lamp lighted from ashes?
For this cause my mind is resolved on this,
To gird my loins with the Magian girdle.[1]
Not for this cause that I may gain fame,
That I have, but am ashamed of it.[2]
Since my rival is base for this cause,
My obscurity is preferable to his fame.
Again an inspiration came to me from "The Truth,"
"Cavil not at Wisdom because of a fool."[3]
If there were no sweepers in the world,
The world would be buried in dust.
After all, the bond of genus connects us all—
So goes the world, *Allah is all-wise.*
Nevertheless flee from the society of the base,
If you seek to be a true servant abandon form;[4]
Form accords not with true obedience,
Practise true obedience, and abandon form.

INDICATION

ON CHRISTIANITY.

In Christianity the end I see is purification from self,[5]
Deliverance from the yoke of bondage.[6]

[1] *I.e.*, as a mark of distinction from the ignorant Shaikh, who cleaves only to outward form. L.

[2] Because it is shared with the ignorant Shaikh. L.

[3] Because all things are created for some purpose. L.

[4] *'Ibadat*, servitude, obedience, devotion. *'Adat*, custom, usage, habit, form, mechanical religion, routine. Lahiji explains it as 'the five pillars' of the Moslem law, viz. reciting the creed, prayer, fasting, alms and pilgrimage. St. Paul's 'righteousness of the law.'

[5] Purification from self, *tajrid*. See note on couplet 86. So in couplet 936 below, purified, *mujarrad*:

"If you ascend, like Messiah, pure and free to heaven."

Hafiz.

[6] Bondage, *taklid*. See note on couplet 109.

The blessed portal of Unity is the sanctuary of the soul,
Which is the nest of the Everlasting—the Simurg.
This doctrine was taught by God's spirit (Jesus),
Who proceeded from the Blessed Spirit.[1]
Also by God is placed in you a soul,
Wherein is a sample of the Blessed Spirit.
If you find release from the carnal mind of humanity,
You will obtain entrance to the life of Divinity.
Every man who is purified as angels are pure
Will ascend with God's spirit to the fourth heaven.

Illustration.[2]

The infant that sucks the breast is confined
At his mother's side in a cradle.
But when he is grown up and able to travel,
If he is manly he goes with his father.
The elements are to you as your mother after the flesh,
You are an infant, and your father is the Father on high.[3]
For this cause said Jesus at the time of His ascension,
"I go unto my Father which is on high."[4]
You too, O soul of your Father, turn to your Father,
Your companions are gone, go forth too.
If you desire to take wing as a bird,
Cast the carrion world to the vultures.
Give to the base the treacherous world,
It is not meet to give carrion but to dogs.[5]
What matters relationship? Seek your real friend,

The Holy Ghost, or "Blessed Spirit," is by Muhammadans identified with the
l Gabriel, the Divine Messenger. See Deutsch, Remains, p. 80, and Koran,
II. 81, III. 40. The Jewish expositors seem to have held the same view.
well *sub loco*.

On the spiritual ascension of the human soul.

Father *ába*. See Rom. viii. 15.

See John xx. 17.

Alluding to the *Hadis*: "The world is carrion, and they that seek it are dogs."

Set your face towards "The Truth," forsake relations.[1]
945 For him who is drowning in the sea of not being,
The text "*no relation*"[2] is the coin of his state.
Every relationship that arises from lust
Yields no issue but pride and high-mindedness.
If lust remained not in the midst,
All relations would become an empty tale.
When lust is doing its work in the midst,
One becomes a father, another a mother.
I say not what your father and mother are,
For it behoves you to regard them with reverence.
950 The deficient in sense is called sister,[3]
The envious is named brother.
Your own enemy is called your son,[4]
And a stranger your kinsman.
Say then who are your paternal and maternal uncles,
What proceeds from them but pain and wrinkles?
The companions who are with you on the mystic path,
O brother, are also companions in foolish jesting.[5]
If you sit in the street of their pleasantry,
What good can I say you see of them?
955 All relations are a fairy tale, a spell, a bond,
By the soul of the prophet they are naught but a delusion.
With manliness deliver yourself like a valiant man,
But yet make not vain the truth of any.[6]
If one atom of the law be neglected,
You will be excluded from the faith in both worlds.
Beware! Omit not the duties of the law,
But at the same time have regard to yourself.

[1] Jesus had no relations says Lahiji, possibly alluding to Matt. xii. 48.

[2] "When the trumpet shall be sounded, there shall be no relation between th on that day, neither shall they ask aid of one another."—Koran, *Sura* XXIII. 10

[3] See couplet 186.

[4] Koran, *Sura* LXIV. 14: "Verily in your wives and children you have enemi

[5] Even the relationship of the Sufi *tarikat* must be renounced. L.

[6] Compare Tennyson, "In Memoriam," xxxiii.

From gold and women[1] comes naught but store of pain,
Abandon them as Jesus abandoned Mary.
Be a "*true believer*,"[2] and forsaking the bond of sects,
Enter the cloister of faith as a Christian monk.[3]
While "other" and "others" are set before your eyes,
Though you be in a mosque, it is no better than a Christian cloister.
When the vesture of "other" passes out of sight,
The cloister becomes to you as a mosque.[4]
I know not in what religious state you are,
Cast out your adversary the flesh, that you may escape.
Idols, girdles, Christianity and church bells
All indicate the renouncing of name and fame.
If you would become a faithful servant,
Prepare yourself in faithfulness and sincerity.
Go, take yourself out of your own road,
Every moment renew your faith.
While infidelity dwells in your inmost soul,
Be not satisfied with this outward Islam.
Of yourself every moment renew your faith,
Be a believer, Be a believer, Be a believer!
Verily faith is born of infidelity,
That is not infidelity from which faith is increased.
Abandon study to be seen and heard of men,

[1] Hammer reads *sozan*, needle, and says there is a legend that Jesus at the time his ascension had a needle stuck in the border of his garment, and could not obtain trance to heaven till he had cast it away.

[2] "Abraham was neither a Jew nor a Christian, but he was of the true religion, a e believer (*Hanifun Muslimun*), and not one of the idolators."—Koran, *Sura* III. This "religion of Abraham" is, according to Deutsch (Remains, pp. 94, 128), clue to Islam. The Hanifs, mentioned in the Talmud, seem to have instructed uhammad in the Jewish faith and doctrines.

[3] *I. e.* renouncing all worldly relations. L.

[4] Koran, *Sura* II. 59: "Verily Muslims and Jews and Christians and Sabeites— oever of these believeth in God and the last day, and doeth that which is right, ll have his reward with the Lord." Compare Acts x. 35: "In every nation he at feareth Him and worketh righteousness is accepted with Him."

Cast off the Durvesh cloak, bind on the Magian girdle.
Be as our Magian sage in pure infidelity,
If you are a man, give your heart to manliness.
Purge yourself from affirmations and negations,
Give your mind wholly to the young Christian.

Indication
of idols and young Christians.[1]

Idols and young Christians are the Light made manifest,
For it finds its exponent in the idol's face.
It leads captive all hearts,
It is now the minstrel,—now the cupbearer.
What a minstrel is he who by one sweet melody
Burns up the garners of a hundred devotees![2]
What a cupbearer is he who by a single cup
Makes drunken two hundred men of threescore and ten!
If he enters the mosque at early dawn,
He leaves not a single wakeful man therein.[3]
If he enters the cloister drunken at night,
He makes Sufis' stories an empty tale.
If he enters the college as a veiled drunkard,
The professor becomes helplessly drunken.
From love to him devotees lost their heads,
And became outcasts from house and home.
He makes one faithful, another an infidel,[4]
He fills the world with tumult and wrong.
Taverns have been edified by his lips,
Mosques have been illumined by his cheek.[5]
All my desire has been accomplished through him,
Through him I gained deliverance from infidel lust.
My heart was hid from knowledge of itself by a hundred veils,

[1] Young Christian, *i.e.* the *Pir* or spiritual guide. L.
[2] *I. e.*, their self regard. L.
[3] They learn their waking to be an 'illusion.' L.
[4] This is the effect of preaching the truth. L.
[5] The tavern is the exponent of the Divine *jalal*, and the mosque of *jamal*. L.

By pride and vanity and self conceit and illusion.
That fair idol entered my door at early morn,
And wakened me from the sleep of negligence.
By his face the secret chamber of my soul was illumined.
Thereby I saw what I myself really am.
When I cast a look on his fair face
I heaved a sigh of wonder from my soul.
He said to me, "O Pharisee and hypocrite,
"Thy life has been spent in seeking name and fame,
"Behold this knowledge, devotion, self seeking and illusion,
"From what have they kept thee back, O laggard!
"To cast one glance on my face for half a moment,
"Is worth a thousand years of devotion."
In fine the face of that world-adorner
Was disclosed and unveiled before my eyes.
The face of my soul was blackened with shame
To think of my life lost and my wasted days.
But when that moon, whose face was as the sun,
Saw that I had cast away hope from my soul,
He filled a goblet and gave it me to drink,[1]
And from that draught fire was kindled within me.
"Now," quoth he, "with this wine, tasteless and odourless,[2]
"Wash from thee the writing on the tablet of Being."
When I had drained that pure draught to the last drop
I fell beside myself on the bare dust.
Now I neither exist in myself, nor do I not exist,
I am not sober, not sick, not drunken.
Sometimes like his eye I am joyful,
Sometimes like his curls I am fluttering.
Sometimes by force of nature I am lying on ashes,
Sometimes at a look from him I am in the rose garden.[3]

[1] The cup of *Ma'rifat*, or Divine knowledge. L.

[2] *I. e.*, pure from phenomenal qualities. L.

[3] This is descriptive of the alternations of *sahu*, sobriety, and *mahu*, intoxication union. L.

EPILOGUE.

1000 From that rose garden I have plucked this posy,
Which I have named "the mystic rose garden."
Therein the roses of hearts' mystery are blooming,
Whereof none has told heretofore.
Therein the tongues of the lilies are all vocal;
The eyes of the narcissus are all far-seeing.
Regard each one with the eyes of the heart
Till your doubts have vanished from before you.
Behold traditional and rational and mystic verities,
Ranged in clear order with knowledge of minutiæ.
1005 Seek not with captious eyes to find blemishes,
For then the roses will turn to thorns in your sight.
Ingratitude is a mark of ignorance,
But knowledge of truth lies in gratitude.
I hope that when the noble[1] calls me to mind,
He may say of me, "*Mercy be upon him.*"
I conclude and end with my own name,
"O Allah, grant me a 'Lauded' end."[2]

[1] '*Azizi.* Tholuck takes this as the titular name (*Takhallas*) of the poet, but it either refers to the noble mentioned in the commencement of the poem or to the pious reader.

[2] *I. e.*, *Mahmud.*

NOTE ON THE PROSODY OF THE "GULSHAN I RAZ."

As before stated (p. v., note), the metre is Hexameter Hazaj Catalectic; the last foot may be *fa'úlun* as well as *mafá'íl.* (Blochmann, Persian Prosody, p. 31.) Though written in the classical period, the poem contains many pre-classic orms, *e.g.* مر before the nominative, l. 755; the *kasra* of the *izáfat* engthened to ی, l. 832; the preposition بر with the *izáfat*, l. 38; را as the ign of the genitive, l. 554; pronominal affixes separated from their verb, . 443; the preposition در placed after its noun, to which بہ is prefixed, . 109. Contractions are frequent, *e.g. bagzasht,* l. 28; *bastad,* l. 61; *anháda,* l. 161; *nabwad,* l. 142; *tust* for *tu ast,* l. 269; *batar* for *badtar,* . 323; *bŭd* for *búd,* l. 914; *arni* for *arini,* l. 193; *alastub rabbakum,* l. 419; a'allallá, l. 13. The *tashdid* of words like حقّ, دقّ, and درّ is dropped f the metre requires it. (Blochmann, p. iv.) The *tashdid* is added b metrum in امّید, l. 821; and, if the readings in the text are correct, o اسم in l. 706, and to بصر and سمع in lines 144 and 403. But this is oubtful. (See Blochmann, p. 9.) In l. 385 the *izáfat* after mute ه is not ounded. (Lumsden, Persian Grammar, ii. 249.) In l. 84 and l. 320 ۀ is reated as a mute ه. In l. 368 and l. 552 ه is treated as an *alif i waçl.* Blochmann, p. 13.) Blochmann says ی doubled by an affixed *izáfat* or ae tankir should not be marked with *hamza,* but the MSS. of this poem nark it with *hamza* or with *tashdid,* as in l. 703; or leave it unmarked, s in ll. 642 and 336. (See Lumsden, ii. 247). Note that *hamza* is often sed when ی is a single vowel, *e. g.* ll. 3 and 435. This, according to Blochmann, is its only correct use with ی. Line 347 will not scan as it tands, but the MSS. offer no alternative reading for تماست. Probably ت here is not sounded, as in کنشت, l. 305, and هفتصد, l. 544. The ISS. generally insert the *hamza,* indicating an *izáfat* or *yae tankir,* after nute ه, but sometimes omit it, as in l. 456.

ERRATA.

Title-page,		*for*	المّلته	*read*	الملّة
Couplet	۲۹	,,	محدّث	,,	محدِث
,,	۴۹	,,	الطف	,,	لطف
,,	۸۱	,,	هست	,,	باشد
,,	۹۰	,,	هیخ	,,	هیچ
,,	۹۸	,,	حق	,,	حَق
,,	۱۰۴	,,	اِحوال	,,	اَحول
,,	۱۴۴	,, بی بصر وبی سمع	adopt marginal reading		
,,	۴۰۳	,,	..	..	..
,,	۱۴۸	,,	پشه	*read*	پشهء
,,	۱۷۹	,,	کنون	,,	اکنون
,,	۱۸۴	,,	برون	,,	بیرون
,,	۱۹۸	,,	رانِي	,,	رَانِي
,,	۲۴۳	,,	ز	,,	زو
,,	۲۶۴	,,	لیک	,,	لیکن
,,	۲۶۹	,,	مضمر	,,	مضمر
,,	۳۰۵	,,	کنشت	,,	کنش
,,	۳۲۱	,,	جز یّات	,,	جزویات
,,	۳۳۱	,,	دار	,,	در
,,	۳۴۶	,,	بآغاز	,,	با آغاز
,,	۳۶۴	Omit *hamza* after دائرة			
,,	۳۶۸	,,	قالو با	,,	قالوا ما
,,	۳۷۶	,,	زد در	,,	زِ دور
,,	۴۲۳	,,	منزّل	,,	منزل

ERRATA.

Couplet	۴۲۶	*for*	رع	*read*	رغ
"	۴۶۱	"	نهاده	"	کرده
"	۴۶۵	"	قالرم	"	قالــزم
"	۴۷۰	"	ندنما	"	نماند
"	۴۷۳	"	فحلوقست	"	مخلوقست
"	۴۸۰	"	هیرلی	"	هیولی
"	۵۰۹	"	کم بیش	"	کم و بیش
"	۵۱۲	"	جز	"	جزء
"	۵۲۷	"	مرکّب	"	مرکب
"	۵۴۴	"	آدرد وگرد تن	"	آورد وگردش
"	۵۴۴	"	هفتصد	"	هفصد
"	۵۴۹	"	محمد	"	با محمد
"	۵۹۲	"	نیکو	"	نکو
"	۶۰۲	"	..	"	..
"	۵۹۳	"	خانه	"	خانهٔ
"	۶۰۲	"	از	"	ز
"	۶۱۱	"	تمثیل	"	بتمثیل
"	۶۶۵	"	از	"	ز *and omit* چون
"	۶۷۰	*Insert nunations after* فان *and* جدید			
"	۷۳۹ (margin)	*for*	لت	*read*	لب
"	۸۲۸	"	دردی	"	دردی

Besides the above errata, د and و have been wrongly interchanged in a few places, *e.g.* ll. 22, 228, 390, 671.

مه از وهم تست این صورت غیر — که نقطه دایرست از سرعت سیر
ی خطست ز اوّل تا بآخر — بر و خلق جهان گشته مسافر
درین ره انبیا چون ساربانند — دلیل و رهنمای کاروانند
ز ایشان سید ما گشته سالار — همو اوّل هم او اخر درین کار
در میم احمد گشته ظاهر — درین دور آمد اوّل عین اخر
احمد تا احد یک میم فرق است — جهانی اندران یک میم غرق است ¹
ر او ختم آمده پایان این راه — بر و منزل شده اُدْعُوا اِلَی اللّٰهِ
قام دلکشایش جمع جمعست — جمال جانفزایش شمع سمعست ²
مده او پیش و دلها جمله درپی — گرفته دست جانها دامنِ وی
رین ره اولیا باز از پس و پیش — نشانی میدهند از منزلِ خویش
ند خویش چون گشتند واقف — سخن گفتند از معروف و عارف
ی از بحر وحدت گفت اَنَا الْحَقّ — یکی از قرب و بعد و سیر زورق
ی را علم ظاهر بوده حاصل — نشانی داده از خشکیِ ساحل
ی گوهر برآورد و هدف شد — یکی بگذاشت آن نزد صدف شد
ی در جزو و کل گفت این سخن باز — یکی کرد از قدیم و محدث اغاز
ی از زلف و خال و خط بیان کرد — شراب و شمع و شاهدرا عیان کرد
ی از هستیِ خود گفت و پندار — یکی مستغرق بُت گشت و زنار
نها چون بوفق منزل افتاد — در افهام خلایق مشکل افتاد
ی کو اندرین معنیست حیران — ضرورت میشود ³ دانستن آن

¹ Omitted by H.
² L. جمعست
³ L. باشدش

سبب نظم کتاب

گذشته هفت و ده از هفتصد سال   ز هجرت ناگهان در ماهِ شوّال
رسولی با هزاران لطف و احسان   رسید از خدمتِ اهل خراسان
بزرگی کاندر انجاهست مشهور   باقسامِ هنر چون چشمهٔ نو
همه اهل خراسان از که و مه   درین عصر از همه گفتند او
نوشته نامهٔ[1] در بابِ معنی   فرستاده بر اربابِ معنی
در آنجا مشکلی چند از عبارات   ز مشکلهای اربابِ اشارا
بنظم آورده و پرسیده یکیک   جهانی معنی اندر لفظ اندک
رسول آن نامه چون برخواند ناگاه   فتاد احوال آن حالی در اف
درآن مجلس عزیزان جمله حاضر   بدین درویش هر یک گشته نا
یکی کو بود مرد کاردیده   ز ما صد بار این معنی شن
مرا گفتا جوابی گوئی در دم   کز انجا نفع گیرند اهل عا
بدو گفتم چه حاجت کین مسائل   نوشتم بارها اندر رسائ
بلی گفتا ولی بروفق مسئول   ز تو منظوم میداریم مأمو
پس از الحاح ایشان کردم آغاز   جواب نامه در الفاظ ایج
بیکلحظه میان جمع[2] احرار   بگفتم این سخن بی فکر و تک
کنون از لطف و احسانی که دارند   ز ما این خرده‌گیها[3] در گذا
همه دانند کین کس در همه عمر   نکرده هیچ قصد گفتن ش
بر آن طبعم اگرچه بود قادر   ولی گفتن نبود الّا بنا

[1] Omitted by H.
[2] L. بسیار
[3] L. خرده گیری

ثر ارچه کتب بسیار می ساخت　　بنظم مثنوی هرگز نپرداخت
وض و قافیه معنی نسنجد　　بهر ظرفی دُر معنی نگنجد
انی هرگز اندر حرف نآید　　که بحر قلزم اندر ظرف نآید
ما از طرف[1] خود در تنگنائیم　　چرا چیزی دگر بر خود[2] فزائیم　　[1] Lo. حرف ؛ [2] Lo. وی
خرست این سخن کز باب شکرست　　بنزد اهل دل تمهید عذرست
از شاعری خود عار نآید　　که در صد قرن چون عطار نآید
رچه زین نمط صد عالم اسرار　　بود یک شمه از دکان عطار
لی این بر سبیل اتفاقست　　نه چون دیو از فرشته استراقست
ی الجمله جواب نامه در دم　　نوشتم[3] یک بیک نه بیش و نه کم　　[3] Lo. بگفتم
سول آن نامه را بستد باعزاز　　و زآن راهی که آمد باز شد باز
ر باره عزیزی کارفرمایی　　مرا گفتا بدان چیزی بیفزایی
ن معنی که گفتی در بیان آر　　ز عینِ علم باعینِ[4] عیان آر　　[4] Lo. در
ی دیدم در اوقات آن مجالی　　که پردازم بدو از ذوق حالی
وصف آن بگفت وگو محالست　　که صاحب حال داند آن چه حالست
لی بر وفق قولِ قائلِ دین　　نکردم ردّ سوال سائلِ دین
لی[5] تاخود شود روشن‌تر اسرار　　در آمد طوطیِ نطقم بگفتار　　[5] Lo. بی ان تاشود
ونِ فضل و توفیق خداوند　　بگفتم جمله را در ساعتی چند
ل از حضرت چونام نامه درخواست　　جواب آمد بدل کان گلشنِ ماست
و حضرت کرد نام نامه گلشن　　شود زو چشم جانها[6] جمله روشن　　[6] Lo. دلها

١ سؤال

L. چه چیز است ١ — نخست از فکر خویشم در تحیّر — که ا چبود آنکه گویندش تفکّ

١ جواب

L. بعالمم ٢ — مرا گفتی بگو چبود تفکّر — کزین معنی فتادم[2] در تحیّ
تفکّر رفتن از باطل سوئی حق — بجزو اندر بدیدن کلّ مطلق
حکیمان کاندرین کردند تصنیف — چنین گفتند در هنگام تعریف
که چون حاصل شود در دل تصوّر — نخستین نام آن شد با تذکّ
وزو چون بگذری هنگام فکرت — بود نام وی اندر عرف عبرت
تصوّر کان بود بهر تدبّر — بنزد اَهل عقل آمد تفکّ
L. ترتیب ٣ — ز تدبیر[3] تصوّرهای معلوم — شود تصدیق نا مفهوم مفهوم
مقدّم چون پدر تالی چو مادر — نتیجه هست فرزند ای برادر
ولی ترتیب مذکور از چه و چون — بود محتاج استعمال قانون
L. ان گره ٤ — دگر باره در او[4] چون نیست تأیید — هر آیینه که هست محض تقلید
ره دور و درازست این رها کن — چو موسی یکزمان ترک عصا کن
در آی در وادیِ ایمن زمانی — شنو إنّي أنا الله بی گمانی
L. وحدت در ٥ — محقّق را که بر وحدت[5] شهودست — نخستین نظرة بر نور وجودست
ولی کز معرفت نورِ صفا دید — ز هر چیزی که دید اوّل خدا دید
L. نور ٦ — بود فکر نکو را شرط تجرید — پس آنگه لمعه از برق[6] تأیید

آنکس را که ایزد راه ننمود   ز استعمال منطق هیچ نگشود

فلسفی چون هست حیران   نمی بیند ز اشیا غیر امکان

مکان میکند اثبات واجب   از آن حیران شد اندر ذات واجب

ی از دوّر دارد سیر معکوس   گهی اندر تسلسل گشته محبوس

عقلش کرد در هستی توغّل   فرو پیچید پایش در تسلسل

ر جمله اشیا بضدّست   ولی حق را نه مانند و نه ندّست

بود ذات حق را ضدّ و همتا   ندانم تا چگونه دانی[1] اورا

د واجب از ممکن نمونه   چگونه دانیش[2] آخر چگونه

نادان که[3] او خورشید تابان   بنور شمع جوید در بیابان

تمثیل

خورشید بر یک حال بودی   شعاع او بیک منوال بودی

ستی کسی کین پرتو اوست   نبودی هیچ فرق از مغز تا پوست

ن جمله فروغ نور حق دان   حق اندر وی ز پیدایست پنهان

ر حق ندارد نقل و تحویل   ندارد[4] اندر او تغییر و تبدیل

اری جهان خود هست[5] دائم   بذات خویشتن پیوسته قائم

کو عقل دوراندیش دارد   بسی سرگشتگی در پیش دارد

وراندیشی عقل فضولی   یکی شد فلسفی دیگر حلولی

نیست تاب نور آن روی   برو از بهر او چشمی دگر جوی

شم فلسفی چون بود احوال   ز وحدت دیدن حق شد معطّل

[1] L. داند
[2] L. داندش
[3] H. omits او.
[4] L. نیابد نور
[5] H. نیست

ز نابینائی آمد رای تشبیه　ز یک چشمیست[١] ادراکات تنز
تناسخ زآن سبب شد کفر و باطل　که آن از تنگ چشمی گشت حا
چو اکمه[٣] بی نصیب از هر کمالست　کسی کورا طریق اعتزالس
رمد دارد دو چشم اهل ظاهر　که از ظاهر نبینند جز مظ
کلامی کو ندارد ذوق توحید　بتاریکی در است از غیم[٤] تق
از و هرچه بگفتند از کم و بیش　نشانی داده اند از دیدهٔ خو
منزه ذاتش از چند و چه و چون　تَعَالَى شَأْنُهُ عَمَّا يَقُول

٢ سؤال

کدامین فکر ما را شرط راهست　چرا که طاعت و گاهی گناه

٢ جواب

در آلا فکر کردن شرط راهست　ولی در ذات حق محض[٥] گناه
بود در ذات حق اندیشه باطل　محالِ محض دان تحصیل حا
چو آیاتست روشن گشته از ذات　نگردد ذات او روشن ز آ
همه عالم بنور اوست پیدا　کجا او گردد از عالم
نگنجد نورِ ذات اندر مظاهر　که سبحات جلالش هست ق
رها کن عقل را با حق همی باش　که تابِ خور ندارد چشم خف
درآن موضع که نور حق دلیل است　چه جائی گفت و گوئی جبرئیل ا
فرشته گرچه دارد قرب درگاه　نگنجد در مقامِ لِي مَعَ

L. چسمی بود ١
H. تنزیه ٢
H. انکس ٣
H. بهم ٤
L. عین ٥
١ Omitted by H.

و نور او فلک را پر بسوزد خردرا جمله پا و سر بسوزد
ود نور خرد در ذات انور بسان چشم سر در چشمهٔ خور
و مُبصَر در بصر نزدیک گردد بصر ز ادراک او تاریک گردد
سیاهی گر بدانی نورِ ذاتست بتاریکی درون آب حیاتست
ـیه جز قابضِ[1] نورِ بصر نیست نظر بگذار کین جای نظر نیست
ـه نسبت خاکرا با عالمِ پاک که ادراکست عجز از درک ادراک
ـیه روئی ز ممکن در دو عالم جدا هرگز نشد وَاللّٰهُ أَعْلَمُ
سواد الوجه فی الدّارین درویش سواد اعظم آمد بی کم و بیش
ـه گویم چونکه هست این نکته باریک شبِ روشن میان روز تاریک
ـر بین مشهد که انوارِ تجلّیست سخن دارم ولی ناگفتن اولیست

تمثیل

ـر خواهی که بینی چشمهٔ خور ترا حاجت فتد با جرم[2] دیگر
ـو چشم سر ندارد طاقت و تاب توان خورشید تابان دید[3] در آب
ـز و چون روشنی کمتر نماید در ادراک تو حالی می فزاید
ـدم آئینه هستی هست مطلق کزو پیداست عکسِ تابشِ حق
ـدم چون گشت هستی را مقابل در و عکسی شد اندر حال حاصل
ـشد آن وحدت ازین کثرت پدیدار یکی را چون[4] شمردی گشت بسیار
ـد گرچه یکی دارد بدایت ولیکن هرگزش نبود[5] نهایت
ـدم در ذات خود چون بود صافی ازو با ظاهر آمد گنج مخفی

[1] H. چون فایض
[2] H. چشم
[3] H. دیدن
[4] H. یکی چون بر
[5] L. نبودش هرگز

حدیث کُنْتُ کَنْزًا را فرو خوان　　که تا پیدا به بینی سرّ پنهان

عدم آئینه عالم عکس و انسان　　چو چشم عکس در وی شخص پنهان

تو چشم عکسی و او نور دیده ست　　بدیده دیده را دیده دیده ست

جهان انسان شد و انسان جهانی　　از این پاکیزه‌تر نبود بیانی

چو نیکو بنگری در اصل این کار　　همو بیننده هم دیده‌ست و دیدا

حدیثِ قدسی این معنی بیان کرد　　و بی بصرُ[1] و بی سمع عیان کر　　(بی بسمع و بی ۱ بصر L.)

جهان را سر بسر آئینه دان　　بهر یک ذره صد مهر[2] پنهان　　(L. تابان ۲)

اگر یک قطره را دل بر شکافی　　برون آید از و صد بحر صافی

بهر جزوی ز خاک ار بنگری راست　　هزاران آدم[3] اندر وی هویداست　　(؟ ادم ۳)

باعضا پشه همچند[4] پیل است　　در اسماء[5] قطره مانند نیل است　　(L. هم وند ۴ — L. اینها ۵)

دل[6] هر حبّه صد خرمن آمد　　جهانی در دل یک ارزن آ　　(L. درون ۶)

به پر پشه درجای[7] جهانی　　درون نقطه چشم آسمانی　　(دریای جای ۷ L.)

بدان خردی که آمد حبّه دل　　خداوند دو عالم راست منزل

در و در جمع گشته هر دو عالم　　گهی ابلیس گردد گاهی آد

ببین عالم بهم[8] درهم سرشته　　ملک در دیو و شیطان در فرشته　　(L. همه درهم ۸)

همه با هم بهم چون دانه و بر　　ز کافر مؤمن و مؤمن ز کا

بهم جمع آمده چون[9] نقطه حال　　همه دورِ زمان روز و مه و سال　　(L. در ۹)

ازل عین ابد افتاده باهم　　نزولِ عیسی و ایجادِ آد

ز هر یک نقطه زین دور مسلسل　　هزاران دور[10] میگردد مشکّل　　(L. شکل ۱۰)

ز هر نقطه چو[11] دوری گشته دایر　　همو مرکز همو در دور سا　　(L. یاه نقطه ۱۱)

ر یک ذرّه را برگیری از جای　　خلل یابد همه عالم سراپای
ه سرگشته و یک جزو از ایشان　　برون ننهاده پا از حدّ امکان
ن هریکی را کرده محبوس　　بجزوّیت ز کلّی گشته مأیوس
گویی دائمًا در سیر و حبسند[1]　　که پیوسته میان خلع و لبسند　　1 جدائند L.
ه در جنبش و دائم در آرام　　نه آغاز یکی پیدا نه انجام
ه از ذات خود پیوسته آگاه　　و ز آنجا راه برده تا بدرگاه
ر پردهٔ هر ذرّه پنهان　　جمالِ جانفزائی روی جانان

قاعده

از عالم همین لفظی شنیدی　　بیا برگو که از عالم چه دیدی
دانستی ز صورت یا ز معنی　　چه باشد آخرت چونست دنیی
و سیمرغ و کوه قاف چبود　　بهشت و دوزخ و اعراف چبود
رامست آن جهان کو نیست پیدا　　که یک روزش بود یک سال[2] اینجا　　2 پنجاه MSS.
مین نبود جهان آخر که دیدی　　نه مَا لَا تُبْصِرُونَ آخر شنیدی
یا بنما که جابلقا کدامست　　جهان[3] شهر جابلسا کدامست　　3 چه ان ?
شارق با مغارب را بیندیش　　چو این عالم ندارد[4] جز یکی بیش　　4 جز omitted H.
یان مَثَلُهُنّ ز[5] ابن عباس　　شنو پس خویشتن را نیک بشناس　　5 بیا بشنو تو این راز H.
در خوابی و این دیدن خیالست　　هرانچه دیدهٔ از وی مثالست
بح حشر چون گردی تو بیدار　　بدانی کین همه وهمست و پندار
و برخیزد خیال چشم احول　　زمین و آسمان گردد مبدّل

چو خورشید عیان بنمایدت چهر — نماند نور ناهید و مه و م
فتد یک تاب ازو بر سنگ خاره — شود چون[۱] پشم رنگین پاره پا
بکن[۲] کنون چو کردن میتوانی — چو نتوانی چه سود[۳] آنگه که دا
چو[۴] میگویم حدیث عالمِ دل — ترا ای سر نشیب و پای در گل
جهان آنِ تو و تو مانده عاجز — ز تو محروم‌تر کس نیست[۵] هرگ
چو محبوسان بیک منزل نشسته — بدست عجز پای خویش بس
نشستی[۶] چون زنان در کوی ادبار — نمیداری ز جهل خویشتن
دلیران جهان آغشته در خون — تو سر پوشیده ننهی پای برو
چه کردی فهم ازین دِین عجائز — که بر خود جهل میداری تو جا
زنان چون ناقصات عقل و دینند — چرا مردان ره ایشان گزین
اگر مردی برون آ[۷] و نظر کن — هر چه آید به پیشت زان گذر ک
میاسا روز و شب اندر مراحل — مشو موقوف همراه و رواحل
خلیل آسا برو حق را طلب کن — شبی را روز و روزی را بشب ک
ستاره با مه و خورشید اکبر — بود حس[۸] و خیال و عقل ا
بگردان زین همه ای راه رو روی — همیشه لَا أُحِبُّ الْآفِلِينَ گو
و یا چون موسیء عمران درین راه — برو تا بشنوی إِنِّي أَنَا ا
ترا تا کوه هستی پیش باقیست[۹] — جواب[۱۰] لفظ أَرِنِي لَنْ تَرَانِيس
حقیقت کهربا ذات تو کاهست — اگر کوه توئی نبود چه راهس
تجلّی کو[۱۱] رشد بر کوه هستی — شود چون خاک ره هستی ز پس
گدائی گردد از یک جذبهٔ شاهی — بیک لحظه دهد کوهی بکا

۱ چشم .H
۲ بدان اکنون که .L
۳ آنرا .H
۴ چه .L
۵ دیده .L
۶ نشسته .H
۷ آی .H
۸ حسن .H
۹ باکی ست .H
۱۰ صد ای .MSS
۱۱ گر رسد .H

...و اندر پی خواجه باسری تفرّج کن همه آیات کبری

...ن آی از سرائی امّهانی بگو مطلق حدیث مَن رَآنی

...اری کن ز کاف کُنج کونین نشین در قاف قرب قابَ قوسَین

...ر حقّ مرترا هر انچه خواهی نمایندت همه اشیا کَمَا هِیَ

قاعدة

...ر انکه جانش در تجلّیست همه عالم کتاب حق تعالیست

...ض اعراب و جوهر چون حروفست مراتب همچو آیات و وقوفست

و هر عالمی چون سوره خاص یکی ز ان فاتحه وان دیگر اخلاص

...ستین آیتش عقل کلّ آمد که دروی همچو بای بسمل آمد

...وم نفس کلّ آمد آیت نور که چون مصباح شد در غایت نور

...وم آیت در وشد عرش رحمان چهارم آیت الکرسی فرو خوان — L. همین

...س از وی جرمهائی اسمانیست که دروی سوره سبع المثانیست

...ر کن باز در جُرم عناصر که هر یک آیتی هستند باهر

...س از عنصر بود جرم سه مولود که نتوان کردن این آیات معدود

...خر گشت پیدا[2] نفس انسان که بر ناس آمد آخر ختم قرآن — [2] L. نازل ...ere H. inserts couplet 488.

قاعدة فی فکر الآفاق

...شو محبوس زندان[3] طبایع برون آی و نظر کن در صنایع — [3] L. ارکان

...فکر کن تو در خلق سموات که تا ممدوح حق کردی[4] بآیات — [4] L. د

ببین یکره که تاخود عرش اعظم　　چگونه شد محیط هر دو عا
چرا کردند نامش عرش رحمان　　چه نسبت دارد او با قلب انسا
چرا در جنبشند این هر دو مادام　　که یک لحظه نمی گیرند آر
مگر دل مرکز عرش بسیط است　　که این چون نقطه آن دور محیط اس
برآید در شبان روزی کم و بیش　　سرا پای تو عرش ای مرد درویش　　L. کمایش [1]　H. رونش [2]
از و در جنبش اجسام مدور　　چرا گشتند یکره نیک بـ
ز مشرق تا بمغرب همچو دولاب　　همی گردند دایم بی خور و خوا
بهر روز و شبی این چرخ اعظم　　کند دور تمامی گرد عا
وزو افلاک دیگرهم بدین سان　　بچرخ اندر همی باشند گردا
ولی بر عکس دور چرخ اطلس　　همی گردند این هشت[3] مقو　　H. مشت [3]
معدل کرسی ذات البروجست　　که او را نه تفاوت نه فروجس
حمل با ثور و با جوزا و خرچنگ　　برو بر همچو شیر و خوشه آونگ
دگر میزان و عقرب پس کمانست　　ز جدی و دلو و حوت انجا نشانس
ثوابت یک هزار و بیست و چارند　　که بر کرسی مقام خویش دا
بهفتم چرخ کیوان پاسبانست　　ششم برجیس را جای و مکانس
بوو پنجم فلک مریخ را جای　　بچارم آفتاب عالم آرا
سوم زهره دوم جای عطارد　　قمر بر چرخ دنیا گشت دا
زحل را جدی و دلو و مشتری باز　　بقوس و حوت کرد انجام ا
حمل با عقرب آمد جای بهرام　　اسد خورشید را شد جای آ
چو زهره ثور و میزان ساخت گوشه　　عطارد رفت در جوزا و خو

ر خرچنگ را هم‌جنس خود دید   ذنب چون رأس شد یک عقده بگزید
ررا بیست و هشت آمد منازل   شود با آفتاب آنگه مقابل
س از وی همچو عرجون قدیمست   ز تقدیر عزیزی کو حکیمست[1]
ر در فکر گردی مرد کامل   هر آئینه بگوئی نیست باطل
ام حقّ همی[2] ناطق بدین است   که باطل دیدن از ضعف یقین[3] است
جود پشه دارد حکمت تام[4]   نباشد در وجود تیر و بهرام
ی چون بنگری در اصل این کار   فلک را بینی اندر حکم جبّار
جم چون ز ایمان بی نصیبست   اثر گوید که[5] از شکل غریبست
ن بیند که این چرخ مدوّر   ز حکم و امر حقّ گشته مسخّر

تمثیل

کوئی هست این افلاک دوّار   بگردش روز و شب چون چرخ فخّار
ز هر لحظهٔ دانای داور   ز آب و گل کند یک ظرف دیگر
انچه در زمان و در مکانست   زیک استاد و از یک کارخانست
کب که همه ز اهل کمالند   چرا هر لحظه در نقص و بالند
در جا و سیر و لون و اشکال   چرا گشتند[6] دائم مختلف حال
گه در حضیض و گه در اوجند   گهی تنها فتاده و گاه زوجند
چرخ از چه شد آخر پر آتش   زشوق کیست آخر[7] در کشاکش
انجم برو گردان پیاده   گهی بالا گهی شیب[8] او فتاده
صر آب و باد و آتش و خاک   گرفته جای خود در زیر افلاک

[1] L. علیم
[2] L. همین
[3] از علتِ ظنین MSS.
[4] L. ای خام
[5] L. از این
[6] L. آخر
[7] L. او اندر
[8] H. وگه نشیب

ملازم[1] هر یکی در منزل[2] خویش — که ننهد پای یک لحظه[3] پس و پیش — L. ملایم ۱ L. مرکز ۲ L. ذره ۳

چهار اضداد در طبع و مراکز — بهم جمع آمده کس دیده هر

مخالف هر یکی در ذات و صورت — شده یک چیز در[4] حکم ضرور — L. از ۴

موالید سه گانه گشت ز ایشان — جماد انگه نبات انگاه حیوا

هیولا را نهاده در میانه — ز صورت گشته فارغ[5] صوفیا — L. صافی ۵

همه از حکم و امر و دادِ داور — بجای ایستاده و گشته مس

جماد از قهر بر خاک اوفتاده — نبات از مهر بر پا ایستا

فروع[6] جانور از صدق و اخلاص — پی ابقای نوع و جنس و اشخا — H. فروع ۶

همه بر حکم داور داده اقرار — مرادررا[7] روز و شب گشته طلب — L. مرادرا ۷

قاعدة الفکر فی آلانفس

باصل خویش یک ره نیک بنگر — که مادر را پدر شد باز ما

جهان را سر بسر در خویش می بین — هر آنچه آید بآخر[8] پیش می بی — H. باول ۸

در آخر گشت پیدا نفس آدم — طفیل ذات او شد هر دو عا

نه آخر علت غائی[9] در آخر — همی گردد بذاتِ خویش ظ — H. غایی ۹

ظلومی و جهولی ضد نورند — و لیک مظهرِ عینِ ظهو

چو پشت آئینه باشد مکدر — نماید روی شخص از روی د

شعاع آفتاب از چارم افلاک — نگردد منعکس جز برسرِ خاک

تو بودی عکس معبود ملائک — از ان گشتی تو مسجودِ ملائک

بود از هر تنی پیش تو جانی — و ز و دربسته با تو ریسما

آن گشتند امرت را مسخّر   که جان هر یکی در تست مضمّر
مغز عالمی زان در میانی   بدان خودرا که تو جان جهانی
ربع شمالی گشت مسکن   که دل در جانب چپ باشد از تن
ان عقل و جان سرمایهٔ تست   زمین و آسمان از سایهٔ[۱] تست
بین آن نیستی کو عین هستیست   بلندی را نگر کو ذات پستیست
یعی قوّت تو ده هزارست   ارادی برتر از حدّ[۲] و شمارست
ان هر یک شده موقوف آلات   ز اعضا و جوارح و ز رباطات
شکان اندرین[۳] گشتند حیران   فرومانند در تشریح انسان
ده هیچکس ره سوی این کار   بعجز خویش هر یک کرده اقرار
حقّ با هر یکی خطّی و قسمیست   معاد و مبدأ هر یک ز اسمیست
ان اسمند موجودات قایم   و زان اسمند در تسبیح دائم
بدأ هر یکی زان مصدری شد   بوقت بازگشتن چون دری شد
آن در کآمد اوّل هم بدر شد   اگرچه در معاش از در بدر شد
آن دانسته تو جمله اسما   که هستی صورت عکس مسمّا
ور قدرت و علم و ارادت   بتست ای بندهٔ صاحب سعادت
یعی و بصیر و حیّ و گویا   بقا داری نه از خود بلکه زآنجا
ی اوّل که عین آخر آمد   زهی باطن که عین ظاهر آمد
از خود روز و شب اندر گمانی   همان بهتر که خودرا می ندانی
و انجام تفکّر شد تحیّر   در اینجا ختم شد بحث تفکّر

۱ پیرایهٔ .L
۲ حصر .H
۳ حکیمان جهان .H
Here H. inserts the couplet repeated at No. 310.
۴ چو .L

۳ سؤال

که باشم من مرا از من خبر کن   چه معنی دارد اندر خود سفر ک

۳ جواب

دگر کردی سوال از من که من چیست   مرا از من خبر کن تا که من کیس
چو هستی مطلق آمد در اشارت   بلفظ من کنند از وی عبار
حقیقت کز[1] تعیّن شد معیّن   تو اورا در عبارت گفتهٔ   H. کزا ۱
من و تو عارض ذات وجودیم   مشبکهای مشکات[2] وجو   L. مشکوا ۲
همه یک نوردان اشباح واَرواح   گه از آینه پیدا گه ز مص
تو گوئی لفظ من در هر عبارت   بسوئی روح می باشد اشار
چو کردی پیشوای خود[3] خرد را   نمی دانی زجزو خویش خو   L. خویش ۳
برو ای خواجه خود را نیک بشناس   که نبود فربهی مانند آما
من و تو برتر از جان و تن آمد   که این هر دو ز اجزای من
بلفظ من نه انسانست مخصوص   که تا گوئی بدو[4] جانست مخصو   L. بدان ۴
یکی ره برتر از کون و مکان شو   جهان بگذار و خود در خود جهان
ز خطِّ وهمی هاء هویّت   دو چشمی میشود در وقت رؤی
نماند در میانه ره رو[5] راه   چو هاء هو شود ملحق   H. ره رو ۵
بود هستی بهشت امکان چو دوزخ   من و تو درمیان مانند بر
چو برخیزد ترا این پرده از پیش   نماند نیز حکم مذهب و ک

... حکمِ شریعت از منِ[1] تست   که آن[2] بربستهٔ جان و تن تست
...ن و تو چون نماند درمیانه   چه مسجد[3] چه کنشت چه دیرخانه
...ن نقطهٔ وهمیست در عین   چو صافی گشت عینت غین شد عین
... خطوه بیش نبود راه سالک   اگرچه دارد او چندین مهالک
... از هایِ هویت درگذشتن   دوم صحرائی هستی در نوشتن[4]
...ین مشهد یکی شد جمع و افراد   چو واحد ساری اندر عین اعداد
...ان جمعی که عین وحدت آمد   تو آن واحد که عین کثرت آمد
...ی این سر شناسد کو گذر کرد   ز جزوی سوی کلی یک سفر کرد

۴ سؤال

...افر چون بود رهرو کدامست   کرا گویم که او مرد تمامست

۴ جواب

... گفتی مسافر کیست در راه   کسی کو شد ز اصل خویش آگاه
...وکش سیر کشفی دان ز امکان   سوی واجب بترک عینِ[5] نقصان
...افر آن بود کو بگذرد زود   ز خود صافی[6] شود چون آتش از دود
...س سیر اوّل در منازل   رود تا گردد او انسان کامل

قاعده

...ن اوّل که تا چون گشت موجود   که تا انسان کامل گشت مولود
... اطوارِ[7] جمادی بود پیدا   پس از روحِ اضافی گشت دانا

1 H. من و
2 H. برشته
3 H. کعبه
4 H. گلشتن
5 L. عین و
6 L. خالی
7 H. اطواری

پس انگه جنبشی کرد او ز قدرت — پس ازوی شد ز حق صاحب ارادت
بطفلی کرد باز احساس عالم — درو بالفعل شد وسواس عالم
چو جزئیات شد بروی مرتب — بکلیات ره برد از مرکب
غضب گشت اندرو پیدا و شهوت — وزایشان خواست بخل و حرص و نخوت
بفعل آمد صفتهای ذمیمه — بتر شد از دد و دیو و بهیمه
تنزل را بود این نقطه اسفل — که شد با نقطهٔ وحدت مقابل
شد از افعال کثرت بی نهایت — مقابل گشت[1] ازین رو با بدایت
اگر گردد مقید اندرین دام — بگمراهی بود کمتر ز انعام
وگر نوری رسد از عالم جان — ز فیض جذبه یا از عکس برهان
دلش با لطف[2] حق همراز گردد — از ان راهی که آمد باز گردد
ز جذبه یا ز برهان یقینی — رهی یابد بایمان یقینی
کند یک رجعت از سجین فجار — رخ آرد سوی علیین ابرار
بتوبه متصف گردد در ان دم — شود در اصطفای ز اولاد آدم
ز افعال نکوهیده شود پاک — چو ادریس نبی در[3] چارم افلاک
چو یابد از صفات بد نجاتی — شود چون نوح از ان صاحب ثباتی
نماند قدرت جزویش در کل — خلیل آسا شود صاحب توکل
ارادت با رضای[4] حق شود ضم — رود چون موسی اندر باب اعظم
ز علم خویشتن یابد رهائی — چو عیسی نبی گردد سمائی
دهد یکباره هستی را بتاراج — در آید از پی[5] احمد بمعراج
رسد چون نقطهٔ اخر باول — در آنجا[6] نه ملک گنجد نه مرسل

L. شد ۱
L. نور ۲
L. آید بر ۳
L. نیابی ۴
H. درولی ۵
L. اندرو ق ۶

تمثیل

...چون افتاب آمد ولی ماه   مقابل گردد اندر لی مع الله
...ت درکمال خویش صافیست   ولایت اندر و پیدا نه مخفیست
...ت در ولی پوشیده باید   ولی اندر نبی پیدا نماید[1]
...ی از پیروی چون همدم آمد   نبی را در ولایت محرم آمد
...ن کنتم تحبّون یابد او راه   بخلوت خانهٔ یحببکم الله
...ان خلوت مرا محبوب گردد   بحقّ یکبارهگی[2] مجذوب گردد
...تابع ولی از روی معنی   بود عابد ولی در کوی معنی
...ی وقتی[3] رسد کارش باتمام   که بآغاز گردد باز انجام

۴ جواب تتمّه

...ی مرد تمامست کز تمامی   کند با خواجگی کار غلامی
...ی آنگاهی که ببرید[4] او مسافت   نهد حقّ بر سرش تاج خلافت
...ی یابد و بعد[5] از فنا باز   رود انجام او[6] دیگر باغاز
...عت را شعار خویش سازد   طریقت را دثار خویش سازد
...قت خود مقام ذات او دان   بود دایم[7] میان کفر و ایمان
...ق حمیده گشته موصوف   بعلم و زهد و تقوی بوده معروف
...با او ولی او زین[8] همه دور   بزیر قبّهای ستر[9] مستور

۱ نماند H.
۲ یکبارگی L.
۳ اگر L.
۴ پوید MSS.
۵ از وصل H.
۶ ره L.
۷ شده جامع L.
۸ از L.
۹ ستّر H.

تمثیل

تبه گردد سراسر مغز بادام   گرش از پوست بخراشی[۱] گه خ
ولی چون پخته شد با پوست[۲] نیکوست   اگر مغزش برآری برکنی پوس
شریعت پوست مغز آمد حقیقت   میان این و آن باشد طریق
خلل در راه سالک نقص مغزست   چو مغزش پخته شد بی پوست نغزس
چو عارف با یقین خویش پیوست   رسیده[۳] گشت مغز و پوست بشکس
وجودش اندر این عالم نپاید   برون رفت او دگر هرگز نیا
دگر با پوست یابد[۵] تابش خور   درین نشأة کند یک دور د
درختی گردد او از آب و از خاک   که شاخش بگذرد[۶] از هفتم افلاک
همان دانه برون آرد[۷] دگر بار   یکی صد گشته از تقدیر جب
چو سیر حبّه در خطّ شجر شد   ز نقطه خطّ[۸] ز خطّ دوری دگر
چو شد در دائره سالک[۹] مکمّل   رسد هم نقطه آخر با
دگر باره شود مانند پرکار   بر آن کاری که اوّل بود درکا
چو کرد او قطع یکباره مسافت   نهد حق بر سرش تاج خلاف
تناسخ نبود این کز روی معنی   ظهوراتست در عین تج
و قد سألوا و قالوا ما النّهایة   فقیل هی الرّجوع الی البد

قاعدة

نبوّت را ظهور[۱۱] از آدم آمد   کمالش در وجود خاتم
ولایت بود باقی تا سفر کرد   چو نقطه در جهان دوری دگر

۱ L. بشکافی
۲ H. بی
۳ L. وسیله
۴ Omitted by H.
۵ L. تابد
۶ H. omits هفتم
۷ L. آید
۸ H. خطی
۹ H. دور
۱۰ L. پر
۱۱ H. omits

ور کلّ او باشد بخاتم   بدو گردد[1] تمامی دور عالم
ور اولیا اورا چو عضوند   که او کلّست و ایشان همچو جزوند
او با خواجه دارد[2] نسبت تام   از و با ظاهر آید رحمت عام
د او مقتدای هر دو عالم   خلیفه گردد از اولاد آدم

تمثیل

نور افتاب از شب جدا شد   ترا صبح و طلوع و استوا شد
ر باره زد در چرخ دوّار   زوال و عصر و مغرب شد پدیدار
ر نور نبی خورشید اعظم   گه از موسی پدید و گه ز آدم
ر تاریخ عالم را بخوانی   مراتب را یکایک باز دانی
خور هردم ظهور سایهٔ شد   که آن معراج دین را پایهٔ شد
ان خواجه خط[3] استوا شد[4]   که او[5] از ظلّ وظلمت مصطفا شد[6]
ط استوا بر قامت راست   ندارد سایه پیش و پس چپ و راست
کرد او برصراط حقّ اقامت   بامر فاستقم میداشت قامت
وش[7] سایه کو دارد سیاهی   زهی نور خدا ظلّ الهی
قبله میان شرق وغربست   ازیرا در میان نور غرقست
ست او چو شیطان شد مسلمان   بزیر پای او شد سایه پنهان
ات جمله زیر پایهٔ اوست   وجود خاکیان از سایهٔ اوست
نورش شد ولایت سایه گستر   مغارب با مشارق شد برابر
ر سایه که اوّل گشت حاصل   در اخر شد یکی دیگر مقابل

۱ یابد L.
۲ یابد L.
۳ وقت L.
۴ بود L.
۵ مکه از هر L.
۶ بود L.
۷ ندارد MSS.

کنون هر عالمی باشد ز امّت   رسولی را[1] مقابل در نبوت
نبی چون در نبوّت بود اکمل   بود از هر ولی ناچار افضل
ولایت شد بخاتم جمله ظاهر   بر اوّل نقطه هم ختم آمد آخر
از[3] و عالم شود پر امن و آمان   نبات و جانور یابد از و جان
نماند در جهان یک نفس کافر   شود عدل حقیقی جمله ظاهر
بود از سرّ وحدت واقفِ حق   در و پیدا نماید وجه مطلق

۵ سؤال

که شد بر سرّ وحدت واقف آخر   شناسای چه آمد عارف آخر

۵ جواب

کسی بر سرّ وحدت گشت واقف   که او واقف نشد اندر مواقف
ولی[4] عارف شناسای وجود است   وجود مطلق او را[5] در شهود است
بجز هستی[6] حقیقی هست نشناخت   و با هستی که هستی[7] پاک در باخت
وجود تو همه خارست و خاشاک   برون انداز از خود جمله را پاک
برو تو خانهٔ دل را فرو روب   مهیّا کن مقام و جای محبوب
چو تو بیرون شدی او اندر آید   بتو بی تو جمالی خود نماید
کسی کو از نوافل گشت محبوب   بلای نفی کرد او خانه جاروب
درون جای محمود او مکان یافت   ز بی بصر و بی[8] سمع نشان یافت
ز هستی تا بود باقی برو شین   نیابد علم عارف صورتِ عین
موانع تا نگردانی ز خود دور   درون خانهٔ دل نایدت نور

1 H. omits را
2 Omitted by H.
3 H. omits و
4 L. دل
5 H. omits را
6 H. هست
7 MSS. دارد
8 L. سمع و بی بصر

چون درین عالم چهارست — طهارت کردن از وی هم چهارست
بن پاکی از احداث و انجاس — دوم از معصیت و ز شر وسواس
م پاکی از اخلاق ذمیمه ست — که با وی آدمی همچون بهیمه ست
م پاکی سرست از غیر — که اینجا منتهی میگردوش سیر
نکو کرد حاصل این طهارات — شود بی شک سزاوار مناجات
ا خودرا بکلی در نبازی — نمازت کی شود هرگز نمازی
ات پاک گردد از همه شین — نمازت گردد آنگه قرة العین
در میانه هیچ تمییز — شود معروف و عارف جمله یک چیز

۶ سؤال

عروف و عارف ذات پاکست — چه سودا در سر این مشت خاکست

۶ جواب

بر نعمت حق نا سپاسی — که تو حق را بنور حق شناسی
معروف و عارف نیست دریاب — ولیکن خاک می یابد ز خور تاب
نبود که دارد ذره امید — هوای تاب مهر و نور خورشید
آور مقام حال فطرت — کز انجا باز دانی اصل فکرت
ت بربکم ایزد چرا[1] گفت — که بود آخر که آن ساعت بلی گفت
ن روزی که گلها می سرشتند — بدل در فیضه[2] ایمان نوشتند
آن نامه را یک ره بخوانی — هر آنچیزی که میخواهی بدانی

1 L. کرا
2 H. قبضه

تو بستی عقد عهد بندگی دوش   ولی کردی بنادانی فراموش
کلام حق بدان گشتست منزل   که با یاوت دهد آن عهد او
اگر تو دیدهٔ حق را بآغاز   در اینجا هم توانی دیدنش
صفاتش را ببین امروز اینجا   که تا ذاتش[1] توانی دید ف   L. ذاتش را ۱
وگر نه رنج خود ضایع مگردان   برو بینوش لایهدی ز قر

تمثیل

ندارد باورت اکمه ز الوان   اگر صد سال گوئی نقل و بر
سفید و زرد و سرخ و سبز و کاهی   بنزد او نباشد جز سیاه
نگر تا کور مادرزاد بدحال   کجا بینا شود از کحل کح
خرد از دیدن احوال عقبی   بود چون کور مادر زاد د
ورای عقل طوری دارد انسان   که بشناسد بدان[2] اسرار پنه   H. بدان سر ۲
بسان آتش اندر سنگ و آهن   نهاده ست ایزد اندر جان و د
چو برهم اوفتاد آن سنگ و آهن   ز نورش هر دو عالم گشت رو
از آن مجموع پیدا گردد این راز   چو بشنیدی برو با خود[3] بپ   H. و با خویش ۳
توئی تو نسخهٔ نقش آلهی   بجو از خویش هر چیزی که خوا

۷ سؤال

کدامین نقطه را نطق است انا الحق   چه گوئی هرزهٔ بود آن مز   MSS. ? مزبحق ۴

۷ جواب

ا الحقّ کشف اسرارست مطلق   بجز حقّ کیست تا گوید انا الحقّ
ـه ذرات عالم همچو منصور   تو خواهی مست گیرو[1] خواه مخمور
ـ ین تسبیح و تهلیلند دائم   بدین معنی همی باشند قائم
ـر خواهی که بر تو[2] گردد آسان   وانْ مِن شَیْءٍ را یکره فرو خوان
ـ کردی خویشتن را پنبه کاری   توهم حلّاج وار این دم براری
ـور پنبهٔ پندارت از گوش   ندای واحد[3] القهّار بنیوش
ـا می آید از حقّ بر دوامت   چرا گشتی تو موقوف قیامت
ـا در وادیِ ایمن که ناگاه   درختی گویدت انّی انا اللّه
ـا باشد انا اللّه از درختی   چرا نبود روا از نیک بختی
ـ آنکس را که اندر دل شکی نیست   یقین داند که هستی جز یکی نیست
ـ نیّت بود حقّ را سزاوار   که هو غیبست و غائب وهم[4] و پندار
ـاب حضرتِ حقّ را دوئی نیست   در آن حضرت من و ما و توی نیست
ـی و ما و تو و او هست یک چیز   که در وحدت نباشد هیچ تمییز
ـ انکو خالی از چون و چرا[5] شد   انا الحقُّ اندر و صوت و صدا شد
ـور با وجه باقی غیر هالک   یکی گردد سلوک و سیر و سالک
ـول و اتّحاد از غیر خیزد   ولی وحدت همه از سیر خیزد
ـبن بود کز هستی جدا شد   نه[6] حقّ بنده نه بنده با خدا شد
ـول و اتّحاد اینجا محالست   که در وحدت دوئی[7] عین ضلالست
ـجود خلق و کثرت در نمودست   نه هر چه آن مینماید عین بودست

۱ L. گیرد
۲ L. گردد بر تو
۳ H. omits ال
۴ H. omits و
۵ L. از خود چون خلا
۶ H. ز
۷ H. روی

تمثیل

بنه آیینه اندر برابر ... در و بنگر ببین آن شخص د
یکی ره باز بین تا چیست آن عکس ... نه اینست و نه آن پس کیست آن عک
چو من هستم بذات خود تعین ... نمیدانم[1] چه باشد سایهٔ م
عدم با هستی اخر چون شود ضم ... نباشد نور و ظلمت هر دو با
چو ماضی نیست مستقبل مه و سال ... چه باشد غیر ازین یک نقطهٔ حال
یکی نقطه اشت وهمی[3] گشته ساری ... تو اورا نام نهاده[4] مهر جار
جز از من[5] اندرین صحرا دگر نیست ... بگو با من که تا صوت و صدا چیس
عرض فانیست جوهر زو مرکب ... بگو کی بود یا خود کو مرکب
ز طول و عرض و[6] ز عمقست اجسام ... وجودی چون پدید آید ز اعد
ازین جنس است اصل جملهٔ عالم ... چو[7] دانستی بیار ایمان[8] فال
جز از حق نیست دیگر هستی الحق ... هو الحق گوی و گر[9] خواهی انا الحق
نمود وهمی از هستی جدا کن ... نه بیگانه خودرا آشنا ک

۸ سوال

چرا مخلوقرا گویند واصل ... سلوک و سیر او چون گشت حاص

۸ جواب

وصال حق ز خلقیت جدا یست[10] ... ز خود بیگانه گشتن آشنایست
چو ممکن گرد امکان بر فشاند[11] ... بجز واجب دگر چیزی ن

[1] L. ندانم تا
[2] H. خال
[3] H. وهم
[4] L. انرا نام کرده نهر
[5] L. بجز من
[6] H. omits
[7] H. کر
[8] H. و فالزم
[9] H گوي تو
[10] H. نیست
[11] H. نشاند

بود هر دو عالم چون خیالست   که در وقت بقا عینِ زوالست
مخلوقست آنکو گشت واصل   نگوید این سَخن را مرد کامل
م کی راه یابد اندر ین باب   چه نسبت خاکرا با ربِّ ارباب
م چبود که با حق واصل آید   و ز و سیر و سلوکی حاصل اید
ر جانت شود زین معنی آگاه   بگوئی در زمان استغفر الله
معدوم و عدم پیوسته ساکن   بواجب کی رسد معدوم ممکن
رد هیچ جوهر بی عرض عین   عرض چبود که لا یبقی زمانین
یمی کاندرین ره[1] کرد تصنیف   بطول و عرض و عمقش کرد تعریف   L. فن ۱
لی چیست جز معدوم مطلق   که میگردد بدو صورت محقق
صورت بی هیولی جز عدم[2] نیست   هیولی نیز بی او جز عدم نیست   L. در قدم ۲
ه اجسام عالم زین دو معدوم   که جز معدوم ازیشان نیست معلوم
بین ماهیتی را بی کم و بیش   نه معدوم و نه موجودست درخویش
ر کن در حقیقت سوی امکان   که بی او[3] هستی آمد عین نقصان   H. بی او که ۳
ود اندر کمالش[4] خویش ساریست   تعیّنها امور اعتباریست   L. کمال ۴
ور اعتباری نیست موجود   عدد بسیار و یکچیزست معدود
انرا نیست هستی جز مجازی   سراسر حال او لهوست و بازی

تمثیل در اطوار وجود

ری مرتفع گردد ز دریا   بامر حق فرو آید بصحرا
اعِ آفتاب از چرخ چارم   فرو بارد[5] شود ترکیب با هم   L. برو افتد ۵

کنند گرمی دگر ره عزم بالا　　در آویزد بدو آن آب د
چو بایشان شود خاک و هوا ضم　　برون آید نباتی[1] سبز و خ　　L. نباتِ ١
غذای[2] جانور گردد بتبدیل　　خورد انسان و یابد باز تحلی　　L. غذاي ٢
شود یک نقطه[3] و[4] گردد در اطوار　　و زآن انسان شود پیدا دگر　　L. نقطه ٣ H. وکرم ٤
چو نور نفس گویا در تن آمد　　یکی جسمِ لطیف و روشن
شود طفل و جوان و کهل و کم پیر　　بداند علم و رأی و فهم و تد
رسد آنگه اجل از حضرت پاک　　رود پاکی بپاک[5] و خاک با خا　　L. بپاکی خاک ٥
همه اجزای عالم چون نباتند　　که یک قطره ز دریای حیا
زمان چون بگذرد بروی شود باز　　همه انجام ایشان همچو آ
رود هر یک از یشان سوی مرکز　　که نگذارد طبیعت[6] جوی　　L. خوی هرگز ٦
چو دریا یست وحدت لیک پرخون　　کز و خیزد هزاران موج مجنو
نگر تا قطرهٔ باران ز دریا　　چگونه یافت چندین شکل وا
بخار و آب و باران و نم و گل　　نبات و جانور و انسانِ کا
همه یک قطره بود اخر در اوّل　　کزو شد این همه اشیا ممتـ
جهان از عقل و نفس و چرخ و اجرام　　چو آن یک قطره دان زاغاز و ا
اجل چون در رسد در چرخ و انجم　　شود هستی همه در نیستی
چو موجی برزند گردد جهان طمس　　یقین گردد که این لم تغن بالام
خیال از پیش بر خیزد بیک بار　　نماند غیر حق در دار
ترا قربی شود آن لحظه حاصل　　شوی بی[7] تو توی با دوست واص　　L. توي ٧
وصال اینجا یگه رفع خیال است　　چو[8] غیر از پیش برخیزد وصال اس　　L. خیال ٨

ممکن ز حدّ خویش بگذشت   نه او واجب شد و نه واجب او گشت

انکو در معانی گشت فایق   نگوید کین بود قلب حقایق

اران نشأه داری خواجه در پیش   برو آمد شد خودرا بیندیش

ث جز[1] و کلّ و نشاء[2] انسان   بگویم یک بیک پیدا و[3] پنهان

۹ سؤال

ال واجب و ممکن بهم چیست   حدیث قرب و بعد و بیش و کم چیست

۹ جواب

ن بشنو حدیث بی کم بیش   ز نزدیکی تو دور افتادی از خویش

هستی را ظهوری در عدم شد   از آنجا قرب و بعد و بیش و کم شد

ب آنست کورا[4] رشّ نورست   بعید آن نیستی کز هست دورست

. نوری ز خود در تو رساند   ترا از هستیِ خود وا[5] رهاند

حاصل مر ترا زین بود و نابود   کز و گاهست[6] خوف و گه رجا بود

بند زو[7] کسی کورا شناسد   که طفل از سایهٔ[8] خود می هراسد[9]

د خوف اگر گردی روانه   نخواهد اسب تازی تازیانه

از آتش دوزخ چه باکست   که از هستی تن و جانِ تو پاکست

آتش زرّ خالص برفروزد   چو غشّی نبود اندر وی چه سوزد

غیر از[10] تو چیزی نیست در پیش   ولیکن از وجود[11] خود بیندیش

ر در خویشتن گردی گرفتار   حجاب تو شود عالم بیکبار

ی در دورِ هستی جزوِ اسفل   توی با نقطهٔ وحدت مقابل

[1] H. جزو و
[2] L. نشات
[3] MSS. ء
[4] L. که کورا
[5] H. خودرا
[6] H. گاهست
[7] H. زکس
[8] H. دایه
[9] H. حراسد
[10] H. omits از
[11] H. omits خود

تعینهای عالم بر تو طاریست — ازان گوئی چو شیطان همچو من کیست
از ان گوئی مرا خود اختیارست — تن من مرکب و جانم سوارست
زمام تن بدست جان نهادند — همه تکلیف بر من زآن نهاد
ندانی کین همه[1] آتش پرستیست — همه این آفت و شوخی ز[2] هستیست
کدامین اختیار ای مرد عاقل[3] — کسی کورا بود بالذات[4] باطل
چو بودِ تست یکسر همچو[5] نابود — بگوئی کاختیارت از کجا بو
کسی کورا وجود از خود نباشد — بذات خویش نیک و بد نباش
کرا دیدی تو اندر هر[6] دو عالم — که یکدم شادمانی یافت بی غ
کرا شد حاصل آخر جمله امید — که ماند اندر کمالی[7] تا بجاو
مراتب باقی و اهل مراتب — بزیر امر حق و الله غالب
موثر حق شناس اندر همه جای — ز حد خویشتن بیرون منه پا
ز حال خویشتن پرس این قدر چیست — و زانجا بازدان کاهل قدر کیس
هر آنکس را که مذهب غیر جبرست — نبی فرمود کو مانند گبرست
چنان کان گبر یزدان اهرمن[8] گفت — همین نادان احمق ما[9] و من گفت
بما افعال را نسبت مجازیست — نسب خود در حقیقت[10] لهو بازیس
نبودی تو که فعلت آفریدند — ترا از بهر کاری برگزید
بقدرت بی سبب دانای[11] برحق — بعلم خویش حکمی کرده مطلق
مقدر گشته پیش از جان و از تن — برای هر یکی کاری معین
یکی هفتصد هزاران سال طاعت — بجا آورد وگرد تن طوق لعن
دگر از معصیت نور و صفا دید — چو توبه کرد و نام اصطفا د

[1] L. ره
[2] L. شومي
[3] L. جاهل
[4] H. omits ل
[5] MSS. مسو
[6] L. جمله
[7] H. علالي
[8] I دمن اگفت
[9] L. او
[10] H. طريقت
[11] L. داراي

...بیتر آنکه این از ترک مأمور — شد از الطاف حق مرحوم و مغفور
...ان دیگر ز منهی[1] گشته ملعون — زهی فعل تو بی چند و چه و چون
...سناب کبریائی لاابالی است — منزه از قیاسات خیالی است
...بود اندر ازل ای مرد نااهل — که این شد محمد و آن ابوجهل
...سی کو با خدا چون و چرا گفت — چو مشرک حضرتش را ناسزا گفت
...را زیبد که پرسد از چه و چون — نباشد اعتراض از بنده موزون
...اوندی همه در کبریائی هست[2] — نه علت لایق فعل خدائی هست[2]
...زاوار خدائی لطف و قهر است[3] — ولیکن بندگی در شکر و[4] صبر است
...امت آدمی را ز اضطراریست — نه[5] آن کورا نصیبی اختیاریست
...دوه[6] هیچ خبرش هرگز از خود — پس آنکه پرسدش از نیک و از بد
...ارد اختیار و گشته مأمور — زهی مسکین که شد مختار و مجبور
...ظلم است این که عین علم و عدلست — نه جور است این که محض لطف و فضلست
...رعت زان سبب تکلیف کردند[7] — که از ذات خودت تعریف کردند[7]
...از تکلیف حق عاجز شوی تو — بیکبار از میان بیرون روی تو
...یت رهائی یابی از خویش — غنی گردی بحق ای مرد درویش
...و جان پدر تن در قضا ده — بتقدیرات یزدانی رضا ده

۱۰ سوأل

...بحر است آنکه نطقش[8] ساحل آمد — ز قعر او چه گوهر حاصل آمد

[1] H. زمنی
[2] H. نیست
[3] H. ش
[4] L. فقر و جبر
[5] H. نه ز
[6] H. نبودش
[7] H. کرده
[8] H. علمش

۱۰ جواب

یکی دریاست هستی نطقِ ساحل   صدف حرف و جواهر دانش دا
بهر موجی هزاران دُرِ شهوار   برون ریزد ز نقل و نصّ و اخبـ
هزاران موج خیزد هر دم از وی   نگردد قطره‌ء هرگز کم از و
H. خلاف ۱ وجود علم از ان دریای ژرفست   غلاف[1] دُرّ آو ازصوت و حرفست
معانی چون کند اینجا تنزّل   ضرورت باشد اورا از تمثّل

تمثیل

شنیدم من که اندر ماه نیسان   صدف بالا رود از بحر عمّار
ز شیب قعر بحر آید بر افراز   بروی بحر بنشیند دهن
بخاری مرتفع گردد ز دریا   فرو بارد بامرِ حقّ تعا
چکد اندر دهانش قطره‌ء چند   شود بسته دهان او بصد
رود با قعر دریا با دلی پُر   شود آن قطره‌ء باران یکی
L. از ۲ بقعر اندر رود غوّاص دریا   و[2] ز و آرد برون لولوء لا
تنِ تو ساحل و هستی چو دریاست   بخارش فیض و باران علم اسماست
خردِ غوّاص این بحر عظیم است   که اورا صد جواهر در گلیم اسـ
H. از ۳ دل آمد علم را[3] مانند یک ظرف   صدف بر علم دل صوتست با حرف
L. با ۴ نفس گردد روان چون برق لامع   رسد ز و حرفها بر[4] گوش سا
صدف بشکن برون کن دُرِّ شهوار   بیفگن پوست مغز نغز بر
لغت با اشتقاق و نحو با صرف   همی گردد همه پیرامن حرف

انکو جمله عمر خود درین کرد — بهرزه صرف عمر نازنین کرد
...رش[1] قشرِ خشک[2] افتاد در دست — بیابد مغز هر کو پوست بشکست — H. زحورش ۱ H. سبز ۲
[3] بی پوست نابختست هر مغز — ز علم ظاهر آمد علم دین نغز — L. ولی ۳
...من جان برادر پند بنیوش — بجان و دل برو در علم دین کوش
...عالم در دو عالم سروری یافت — اگر کمتر[4] بُد از وی مهتری یافت — L. کهتر ۴
...ی کان از سر احوال باشد — بسی بهتر ز علم قال باشد
...ی کاری که از آب و گلِ آمد — نه چون علمست کان کار دل آمد
...ن جسم جان بنگر چه فرقست — که این را غرب گیرد[5] آن چو شرقست — L. گیری ۵
آنجا بار دان احوال اعمال — بنسبت با علوم قال با حال[6] — H. جال ۶
...لمست آنکه دارد میل دنیی — که صورت دارد[7] الّا نیست معنی — L. اما ۷
...رد جمع هرگز علم با آز — ملک خواهی سگ از خود دور انداز
...م دین ز اخلاق فرشتست — نباشد[8] در دلی کو سگ سرشتست — L. نماید ۸
...ث مصطفا آخر همین است — نیکو بشنو که البته چنین است
...ن خانه چون هست صورت — فرشته ناید اندر وی ضرورت
... بزدای روی تختهٔ دل — که تا سازد ملک پیش تو منزل
و تحصیل کن علمِ وراثت — ز بهرِ آخرت میکن حراثت
...ب حق بخوان از نفس و آفاق — مزیّن شو باصل جمله اخلاق

قاعده

در اخلاق و خصال حمیده

...ول[9] خلق نیک آمد عدالت — پس از وی حکمت و عفّت شجاعت — H. اصل ۹

حکیم راست گفتار ست و کردار — کسی کو متصف گردد بدین ج
زحکمت باشدش جان و دل آگه — نه گربزا[1] باشد و نه نیز[2] ا
بعفت شهوت دل[3] کرده مستور[4] — شره همچون خمود[5] از وی شده د
شجاع و صافی از ذل تکبر — مبرا ذاتش از جبن و ته
عدالت چون شعار ذات او شد — ندارد ظلم از ان خلقش نیکو
همه اخلاق نیکو در میان[6] است — که از افراط و تفریطش کرانس
میانه چون صراط المستقیم است — ز هر دو جانبش قعر جحیم اس
بباریکی و تیزی موی[7] و شمشیر — نه روی رفتن[8] و بودن بر و د
عدالت چون یکی دارد ز اضداد — همی هفت آمد این اضداد ز اع
بزیر هر عدد سری نهفتست — از آن درهای[9] دوزخ نیز هفتس
چنان کز ظلم شد دوزخ مهیا — بهشت آمد همیشه عدل را
جزای عدل نور و رحمت آمد — جزای[10] ظلم لعن و ظلمت آ
ظهور نیکوئی در اعتدالست — عدالت جسم را[11] اقصی الکمالس
مرکب چون شود مانند یک چیز — ز اجزا دور گردد فعل و تم
بسیط الذات را مانند گردد — میان این وآن پیوند گر
نه پیوندی که از ترکیب اجزاست — که روح از وصف جسمیت مبراس
چو آب وگل شود یکباره صافی — رسد از حق بدو روح اضاف
چو یابد تسویت اجزای و ارکان — در و گیرد فروغ عالم جا
شعاع جان سوی تن وقت تعدیل — چو خورشید و زمین آمد تمثیا

[1] گربزا H. [2] پهیز H. [3] خود L. [4] مشهور H. [5] حسد H. [6] میانه L. [7] مهو L. [8] گشتن L. [9] در پای H. [10] سزای L. [11] عدل H.

تمثیل

چه خور بچرخ چارمین است   شعاعش نور تدبیر زمین است

...تهای عنصر نزد خور نیست   کواکب گرم وسرد وخشک وترنیست

...ر جمله از وی گرم و سرد است   سفید وسرخ وسبز وآل و زرد ست

حکمش[1] روان چون شاه عادل   که نه خارج توان گفتن نه داخل

...ر تعدیل گشت[2] ارکان موافق   زحسنش نفس گویا گشت عاشق

...ح معنوی افتاد در دین   جهانرا نفس کلّی داد کابین

...یشان می پدید آید فصاحت   علوم و نطق و اخلاص و صباحت

...ت از جهان بی مثالی   در آمد همچو رندِ لا اُبالیِ

...ر مستان نیکوئی عَلَم زد   همه ترتیب عالم را بهم زد

...ی بررخش حسن او شهسوارست   گهی با تیغ نطق آبدار ست

...ور شخص است خوانندش ملاحت   چو[3] در نطقست گویندش فصاحت

...ی و شاه و درویش و پیمبر   همه در تحت حکم او مسخّر

...ن حسن روی نیکو ان چیست   نه آن حسنست تنها گوی آن چیست

... از حق می نیاید دلربائی   که شرکت نیست کس را در خدائی

... شهوت دل مردم رباید   که حق گه گه ز[4] باطل می نماید

...ر حق شناس اندر همه جای   ز حد خویشتن بیرون منه پای

...ی اندر کسوت حق دین حق وان   حق اندر باطل آید کار شیطان

---

[1] ش omitted H.

[2] شد L.

[3] چه H.

[4] ز omitted H.

سوأل

چه جزوست آنکه او از کلّ فزونست　　طریق جُستن آن جزو چون[ست]

جواب

وجود آن جزو دان کز کلّ فزونست　　که موجودست کلّ وین بازگونست
بود موجودرا کثرت برونی　　که او وحدت ندارد جز درون[ی]
L. بود ۱ ؛ H. سائر ۲　وجود کلّ ز کثرت گشت ظاهر　　که او در[۱] وحدت جزوست ساتر[۲]
L. بود ۳　چو کلّ از روی ظاهر هست بسیار　　شود[۳] از جزو خود کمتر بمقد[ار]
نه آخر واجب آمد جزو هستی　　که هستی کرد اورا زیردست[ی]
ندارد کلّ وجودی در حقیقت　　که او چون عارضی شد بر حقیق[ت]
H. وحدت ۴　وجود کلّ کثیر و احد آید　　کثیر از روی کثرت[۴] می نما[ید]
H. ان ۵　عرض شد[۵] هستی کان اجتماعیست　　عرض سوئی عدم بالذّات ساعیس[ت]
L. زهر ۶　بهر[۶] جزوی ز کلّ کان نیست گردد　　کلّ اندر دم ز امکان نیست گر[دد]
جهان کلّست و در هر طرفة العین　　عدم گردد و لا یبقی زمانی[ن]
دگر باره شود پیدا جهانی　　بهر لحظه زمین و آسما[نی]
L. ساعت ۷ ؛ H. حشري ۸　بهر لحظه[۷] جوان این کهنه پیرست　　بهردم اندر و حشر و[۸] بشیرس[ت]
درو چیزی دو ساعت مینپاید　　در آن لحظه که می میرد بز[اید]
ولیکن طامة الکبری نه اینست　　که این یوم عمل وآن یوم دینس[ت]
L. گرفتار ۹　از ان تا این بسی فرقست زنهار　　بنادانی مکن خودرا ز[۹] کفتا[ر]
نظر بکشای در تفصیل و اجمال　　نگر در ساعت و روز و مه و سا[ل]

تمثیل

ر خواهی که این معنی بدانی   ترا هم هست مرگ و زندگانی
رچه اندر جهان از شیب[1] و بالاست   مثالش در تن و جان تو پیداست
ان چون تست یک شخص معین   تو اورا گشته چون جان او تراتن
گونه نوع انسان را مماتست   یکی هر لحظه وان بر حسب ذاتست
[2] دیگر دان ممات اختیاریست   سیوم مردن مرورا[3] اضطراریست
و مرگ و زندگی باشد مقابل   سه نوع آمد حیاتش در سه منزل
انرا نیست مرگ اختیاری   که این را از همه عالم تو داری
ی هرلحظه میگردد مبدل   در آخر هم شود مانند اول
آنچه آن گردد اندر حشر پیدا   ز تو در نزع میگردد هویدا
تو چون زمین سر آسمانست   حواست[4] انجم و خورشید جانست
وهست استخوانهائی که سختست   نباتت موی و اطرافت درختست
ت در وقت مردن از ندامت   بلرزد چون زمین روز قیامت
اغ آشفته و جان تیره گردد   حواست همچو انجم خیره گردد
امات گردد از خوی همچو دریا   تو در وی غرقه گشتی بی سر و پا
د از جان کنش ای مرد مسکین   از سستی استخوانها[5] چون پشم رنگین
م پیچیده گردد ساق با ساق   همه جفتی[6] شود از جفت[6] خود طاق
روح از تن بکلیت جدا شد   زمینت قاع صفصف لا تری شد
ن منوال باشد کار عالم   که تو در خویش می بینی در آندم
حقست و باقی جمله فانیست   بیانش[7] جمله در سبع المثانیست

1 L. نثر
2 L. دوم زانها
3 L. مر اورا
4 H. inserts موی
5 H. کوه ها
6 H. خفت
7 H. بنامش

چو کلّ مَنْ علیها فان بیان کرد — لفي[1] خلقٍ جدید هم عیان کرد — MSS. تبس ۱

بود ایجاد و اعدام دو عالم — چو خلق و بعث نفس ابن آدم

همیشه خلق در خلق جدید است — اگرچه مدت عمرش مدید است

همیشه فیض فضل حقّ تعالی — بود در[2] شأن خود اندر تجلّی — L. از ۲

از آنجانب[3] بود ایجاد و تکمیل — و زینجانب بود هرلحظه تبدیل — H. انجا ۳

ولیکن چون گذشت این طور دنیا — بقای کلّ بود در روز عقبی

که هر چیزی که بینی بالضرورة — دو عالم دارد از معنی و صورت

وصالِ اوّلین عینِ فراقست — مران دیگر ز عند الله باقست

بقا اسم وجود آمد و لیکن — بجائی کو[4] بود سایر چو ساکن — L. کان ۴

مظاهر چون فتد بر وفق ظاهر — در اوّل مینماید عین آخر

هر آنچه هست بالقوة درین دار — بفعل آمد در ان عالم بیکبار

قاعده

ز تو هر فعل کاوّل گشت ظاهر — بران گردی بباری چند قادر

بهر باری[5] اگر نفعست وگر[6] ضر — شود در نفس تو چیزی مدخر — H. باری ۵; H. اگه ۶

بعادت حالهای با خوی گردد — بمدّت میوها خوشبوی گردد

از آن آموخت انسان پیشهها را — و ز آن ترکیب کرد اندیشهها را

همه افعال و اقوال مدّخر — هویدا گردد اندر روز محشر

چو عریان گردی از پیراهن تن — شود عیب و هنر[7] یکباره روشن — H. هر ۷

تنت باشد و لیکن بی کدورت — که بنماید ازو چون آب صورت

همه پیدا شود آنجا ضمائر — فرو خوان آیت تبلی السّرائر

بر باره بوفق عالمِ خاص   شود اخلاقِ[1] تو اجسام و اشخاص   اخلاص .H

بنان کز قوت[2] عنصر درین جا   موالید سه گانه گشت پیدا   وقت .H

مه اخلاق تو در عالمِ جان   گهی انوار گردد گاه نیران

عین مرتفع گردد ز هستی   نماند در نظر بالا و پستی

اند مرگ تن در دار حیوان   بیک رنگی برآید قالب و[3] جان   و omitted. H.

در پا و سر تو جمله[4] چون دل   شود صافی ز ظلمت صورت گل   و چشم تو .L

بینی بی جهت حق را تعالی   کند از[5] نور حق بر تو[6] تجلّی   هم .L خود .H In this and the next couplet the order of the lines is inverted by L.

ندانم تا چه مستیها کنی تو   دو عالم را همه[7] برهم زنی تو   همی .H

سقاهم ربّهم چه بود بیندیش   طهوراً چیست صافی گشتن از خویش

زهی لذت زهی دولت زهی ذوق   زهی حیرت زهی حالت زهی شوق *

خوشا آندم که ما بی خویش باشیم   غنیء مطلق و درویش باشیم

دین نه عقل نه تقوی نه ادراک   فتاده مست و حیران بر سرِ خاک

بهشت و خلد و حور انجا چه سنجد   که بیگانه[8] در آن خلوت نگنجد   بیگان .H

چو رؤیت دیدم و خوردم ازان[9] می   ندانم تا چه خواهد شد پس از وی   دمی .H

ی[10] هر مستی[11] باشد خماری   درین اندیشه دل خون گشت باری   وي .H مستي .H

سوأل[12]

قدیم و محدث از هم[13] چون جدا شد   که این عالم شد آن دیگر خدا شد   خود .H

جواب[12]

قدیم و محدث از هم خود[14] جدا نیست   که از هستیست باقی دائما نیست   چون .H

* L. زهي شربت زهي لذت زهي ذوق   زهي دولت زهي حيرت زهي شوق

همه آنست و این مانند عنقاست　　جز از حق جمله اسم بی مُسماست

[H. وجود ۱] عدم موجود گردد این محالست　　وجود[1] از روی هستی لا یزالست

ز آن این گردد و نه این شود آن　　همه اشکال گردد بر تو آسان

جهان خود جمله امرِ اعتباریست　　چو آن یک نقطه کاندر دور ساریست

برو یک نقطهٔ آتش بگردان　　که بینی دائره از سرعتِ آن

[H. گردد ۲] یکی گر در[2] شمار آید بناچار　　نگردد واحد از اعداد بسیار

حدیث ما سوی الله را رها کن　　بعقل خویش آنرا زین جدا کن

[H. روی ۳] چو شک داری درآن کین چون خیالست　　که با وحدت دوی[3] عین ضلالست

عدم مانند هستی بود یکتا　　همه کثرت ز نسبت گشت پیدا

ظهور اختلاف و کثرت شأن　　شده پیدا ز بوقلمون امکان

وجود هر یکی چون بود واحد　　بوحدانیت حق گشت شاهد

۱۳ سؤال

چه خواهد مرد معنی ز آن عبارت　　که دارد سوی چشم و لب اشارت

[H. سر ۴] چه جوید از رخ و[4] زلف و خط و خال　　کسی کاندر مقاماتست و احوال

۱۳ جواب

هر آن چیزی که در عالم عیانست　　چو عکسی ز آفتاب آن جهانست

جهان چون زلف و خطّ و خال و ابروست　　که هر چیزی بجای خویش نیکوست

تجلی گه جمال و گه جلالست　　رخ و زلف آن معانی را مثالست

صفات حق تعالی لطف و قهرست　　رخ و زلف بتانرا ز آن دو بهرست

محسوس آمد این الفاظ مسموع   نخست از بهر محسوسند[1] موضوع   H. مخصوصت [1]

رد عالم معنی نهایت   کجا بیند مراورا[2] لفظ و غایت   H. مرادا [2]

آن معنی که شد بر ذوق پیدا   کجا تعبیر لفظی یابد اورا

اهلِ دل کند تفسیر معنی   بمانندی کند تعبیر معنی

محسوسات از آن عالم چو سایه است   که این چون طفل وآن مانند دایه است

رد من خود الفاظِ ماوّل   بر آن معنی فتاد از وضع اوّل

سوسات خاص از عرف عام است   چه داند عام کان معنی کدام است

ر چون در جهان عقل کردند   از آنجا لفظها را نقل کردند

سب را رعایت کرد[3] عاقل   چو سوی لفظ ومعنی گشت نازل   H. گردد [3]

ی تشبیه کلّی نیست ممکن   زجست و جوی آن می باش ساکن

ین معنی کسی را بر تو دق نیست   که صاحب مذهب اینجا غیر حق نیست

ی تا با خودی زینهار زینهار   عبارات شریعت را نگه دار

رخصت اهل دل را در سه حالست   فنا و سکر و پس[4] دیگر دلالست   H. شکر سه [4]

چون[5] نیست احوالِ[6] مواجید   مشو کافر بنادانی و تقلید   L. گر [5] H. افعال [6]

آنکس کو شناسد این سه حالت   بداند وضع و الفاظ و دلالت

ازی نیست احوالِ حقیقت   نه هر کس یابد اسرار حقیقت[7]   H. طریقت [7]

ف ای دوست ناید ز اهل تحقیق   مر این را کشف باید یا که[8] تصدیق   H. نه [8]

فتم وضع الفاظ و معانی   ترا سربسته گر داری بدانی

ر کن در معانی سوی غایت   لوازم را بیکایک کن رعایت

جهی خاص از ان تشبیه میکن   ز دیگر وجهها تنزیه میکن

چو شد این قاعده یکسر مقرّر نمایم ز آن مثالی چند دیگر

اشارت بچشم و لب

نگر کز چشم شاهد چیست پیدا رعایت کن لوازم را بدانجا
ز چشمش خواست[۲] بیماری و مستی زلعلش گشت[۳] پیدا عین هستی
ز چشم او همه دلها جگرخوار لب لعلش شفای جان بیمار
زچشم اوست دلها مست و مخمور ز لعل اوست جانها جمله مستو
بچشمش گرچه عالم در نیاید لبش هر ساعتی لطفی نماید
دمی از مردمی دلها نوازد دمی بیچارگان را چاره سازد
بشوخی جان دهد در آب و در خاک بدم دادن زند آتش بر افلاک
از و هر غمزه دام و دانهٔ شد و ز و هرگوشه میخانهٔ شد
ز غمزه میدهد هستی بغارت ببوسه میکند بازش عمارت
زچشمش خون ما در جوش دایم ز لعلش جان ما بیهوش دایم
بغمزه چشم او دل می رباید بعشوه لعل او جان می رباید
چو از چشم و لبش خواهی[۴] کناری مراین گوید که نه آن گوید آری
ز غمزه عالمی را کار سازد ببوسه هر زمان جان می نوازد
از ویک غمزه و جان دادن از ما و ز ویک بوسه و استادن از ما
کلمح[۵] بالبصر شد حشر عالم ز نفخ روح[۶] پیدا گشت آدم
چو از چشم و لبش اندیشه کردند جهانی می پرستی پیشه کردند
نیاید در[۷] دو چشمش جمله هستی در و چون آید آخر خواب مستی

MS ۱ وازلت
H. ۲ خاست
۳ درتست مستي
MS هستي
L. ۴ جوي
H. ۵ زلمه
E ۶ نفخ صور
۷ ی در نیاید
L.

...رد ما همه مستیست یا خواب — چه نسبت خاک را با ربّ ارباب
...ر دارد ازین صد گونه اشفت[1] — که وَلتصنَع علی عینی چرا گفت

اشارت بزلف

...یت زلف جانان بس درازست — چه شاید گفت ازان[2] کان جای رازست[3]
...بس از من حدیث زلفِ بر چین — مجانین زنجیر [?] محبّا بند[4]
...قدش راستی گفتم سخن دوش — سر زلفش مرا گفتا که خاموش[5]
...ی بر راستی زان گشت غالب — وزو در پیچش[6] آمد راه طالب
...ه دلها از و گشته مسلسل — همه جانها از و گشته[7] مغلغل[8]
...ق صد هزاران دل ز هر سو — نشد یکدل برون از[9] حلقهٔ او
...او[10] زلفین مشکین بر فشاند — بعالم در یکی کافر نماند
...گر بگذاردش پیوسته ساکن — نماند در جهان یک نفس مؤمن
...دام فتنه می شد چنبر او — بشوخی باز کرد از تن سر او
...ر زلفش بریده شد چه غم بود — که[11] گر کم شد شب اندر روز افزود
...او بر کاروانِ عقل ره زد — بدست خویشتن بر وی گره زد
...بد زلف او یک لحظه آرام — گهی بام آورد گاهی کند شام
...وی وزلف خود صد روز وشب کرد — بسی بازیچهای بو العجب کرد
...ن آدم در آن دم شد مخمّر — که دارد[12] بوی آن زلفِ معطّر[13]
...ن ما دارد از زلفش نشانی — که خود ساکن نمیگردد زمانی
و هرلحظه کار از سر گرفتم — ز جان خویشتن دل بر گرفتم

[1] اشگفت H.
[2] ان omitted. H.
[3] روز H.
[4] بجنبانید MSS. مجتّابند H ?
[5] فرو پوش H.
[6] پیش H.
[7] بوده L.
[8] مقلقل H.
[9] خلقه H.
[10] اگر زلفین خودرا L.
[11] نه H.
[12] دادش L.
[13] معبیر L.

از آن گردد دل از زلفش مشوّش　　که از رویش دلی دارد بر آتش

اشارت برخ و خط

رخ اینجا مظهر حسن خدائیست　　مراد از خط جناب کبریائیست
رخش خطّی کشید اندر نکوئی　　که از ما نیست بیرون خوب روئی
خط آمد سبزه زارِ عالمِ جان　　از آن کردند نامش آب[1] حیوان　　L. دار [1]
ز تاریکیء زلفش روز شب کن　　ز خطّش چشمهء حیوان طلب کن
خضروار از مقام بی نشانی　　بخور[2] چون خطّش[3] آب زندگانی　　H. بخود [2] H. خضر [3]
اگر روی و خطّش بینی تو بیشک　　بدانی کثرت از وحدت یکایک
ز زلفش باز دانی کار عالم　　ز خطّش باز خوانی سرّ مبهم
کسی گر[4] خطّش از روی نکو دید　　دلِ من روی او در خطِّ او دید　　L. کو [4]
مگر رخسار او سبع المثانیست　　که هر حرفی از و بحرِ معانیست
نهفته زیر هر موئی از[5] و باز　　هزاران بحرِ علم از عالم[6] راز　　[5] عالم inserted. H. [6] عالم omitted H.
ببین بر آب قلبِ عرشِ رحمان　　ز خطِّ عارضِ زیبائی جانان

اشارت بخال

بر آن رخ نقطهٔ خالش بسیط است　　که اصل مرکزِ دورِ محیط است
از و شد خطّ دور هر[7] دو عالم　　و زو شد خطّ نقشَ قلب آدم　　[7] هر omitted. H.
از آن حالِ دلِ پر خون تباهست　　که عکس نقطهء خال سیاهست
چو[8] خالش حال دل جز خون شدن نیست　　کز آن منزل رهِ بیرون شدن نیست　　L. ز [8]
بوحدت در نباشد هیچ کثرت　　دو نقطه نبود اندر اصل وحدت

م خال او عکس دل ماست — و یا دل عکس خال روی زیباست

عکس خال او دل گشت پیدا — و یا عکس دل آنجا شد هویدا

ی اندر روی او یا اوست[1] در دل — بمن پوشیده گشت[2] این راز مشکل

هست این دل ما[3] عکس آن خال — چرا می باشد آخر مختلف حال

ی چون چشم مخمورش خرابست — گهی چون زلف او در اضطرابست

ی روشن چو آن روی چو ماهست — گهی تاریک چون خالِ سیاهست

ی مسجد بود گاهی کنشت است — گهی دوزخ بود گاهی بهشت است

ی برتر شود از هفتم افلاک — گهی افتد بزیر توده[4] خاک

ی از زهد و ورع گردد دگر بار — شراب و شمع و شاهد را طلبکار[5]

سوال ۱۴

ب و شمع و شاهد را چه معنیست — خراباتی شدن آخر چه دعویست

جواب ۱۴

ب و شمع و شاهد عین معنیست — که در هر صورتی او را تجلّیست

ب و شمع نور و ذوق عرفان — به[6] بین شاهد که از کس نیست پنهان

ب اینجا زجاج شمع مصباح — بود شاهد فروغ نور ارواح

شاهد بر دل موسی شرر شد — شرابش اتش و شمعش شجر شد

ب و شمع جان آن نور اسری[7] است — ولی شاهد همان آیاتِ کبری است

ب و شمع و شاهد جمله حاضر — مشو غافل ز شاهد بازی آخر

ب بیخودی درکش زمانی — مگر از دست خود یابی امانی[8]

[1] روي H.
[2] شد L.
[3] ما omitted. H.
[4] دوده H.
[5] H. omits this couplet.
[6] وسکر H.
[7] اشراست MSS.
[8] آماني H.

بخور می تا ز خویشتن وارهاند — وجود قطره در دریا ر

شرابی خور که جامش روی یارست — پیاله چشم مست باده خوار

شرابی را[1] طلب بی ساغر وجام — شرابی باده خوار و ساقی آ

شرابی خور ز جام وجه باقي — سقاهم ربّهم اوراست س

طهوراً می[2] بود کز لوث هستی — ترا پاکی دهد در وقت

بخور می وارهان خودرا ز سردی — که بدمستی بهست از نیک

کسی کو افتد از درگاه حق دور — حجاب ظلمت اورا بهتر از

چو[3] آدم را ز ظلمت صد مدد شد — ز نور ابلیس ملعونِ ابد

اگر آئینهٔ دل را زدودست — چو خودرا بیند اندر وی چه سود

ز رویش پرتوی چون بر می افتاد — بسی شکل حبابی بر وی ا

جهان و[4] جان در و شکل حبابست — حبابش اولیائی را قبا ب

شده ز و عقل کل حیران و مدهوش — فتاده نفس کل را[5] حلقه در گ

همه عالم چو یک خمخانهٔ اوست — دل هر ذرّهٔ پیمانهٔ او

خرد مست و ملائک مست و[6] جان مست — هوا مست و زمین مست آسمان

فلک سرگشته از وی در تکاپوی — هوا در دل باميدِ یکی

ملائک خورده صاف از کوزهٔ پاک — بجرعه ریخته دردی[7] برین خ

عناصر گشته زان یک جرعه سرخوش — فتاده گه در آب و گه در ا

ز بوی جرعهٔ کافتاد[8] بر خاک — بر آمد آدمی تا شد بر اف

زعکسِ او تن پژمرده جان گشت — زتابش جانِ افسرده روان گ

جهانی[9] خلق از و سرگشته دایم — ز خان و مان خود برگشته

[1] H. omits this couplet.
[2] می omitted. H.
[3] گر L.
[4] و omitted. H.
[5] در حلقهٔ گوش H.
[6] و omitted. H.
[7] دردي H.
[8] افتاده H.
[9] جهان H.

از بوی دُردش عاقل آمد   یکی از رنگ صافش ناقل آمد
از نیم جرعه گشته صادق   یکی از یک صراحی گشته عاشق
دیگر فرو بُرده بیک بار   خم[1] و خمخانه و ساقی و میخوار
ه جمله و مانده[2] دهن باز   زهی دریا دلِ رندِ سرافراز
اشامیده هستی را بیک بار   فراغت یافته ز اقرار و انکار
فارغ ز زهد خشک و طامات   گرفته دامنِ پیرِ خرابات

اشارت بخراباتیان

تی شدن از خود رهائیست   خودی کفرست اگر خود پارسائیست[3]
ی داده اندت از خرابات   که التّوحیدُ اسقاط الاضافات
ت از جهانِ بی مثالیست   مقامِ عاشقانِ لا اُبالیست
ت آشیان مرغ جانست   خرابات آستان لامکانست
تی خراب اندر خراست   که در[4] صحرای او عالم سرابست
تیست بی حدّ و نهایت   نه آغازش کسی دیده نه غایت
صد سال در وی می شتابی   نه خود را و نه کس[5] را باز یابی
ی اندر و بی پا و بی سر   همه نه مؤمن و نه نیز کافر
ب بیخودی در سر گرفته   بترک جمله خیر و شر گرفته
ی خورده هریک بی لب و کام   فراغت یافته از ننگ و از نام
ث ماجرای شطح و طامات   خیال خلوت و نور و کرامات
ی دُردی از دست داده   ز ذوقِ نیستی مست اوفتاده
و رکوه و تسبیح و مسواک[6]   گرو کرده[7] بدُردی جمله را پاک[8]

[1] H. می
[2] H. ماند دهان
[3] H پارسا نیست
[4] H. و
[5] H. عش
[6] H. زنّار
[7] H. گزد
[8] H. یکبار

میان آب و گل افتان و خیزان　　بجای اشک خون از دیده ر
دمی[1] از سرخوشی درعالم ناز[2]　　شده چون شاطران گردن ا
گهی از رو سیاهی رو بدیوار　　گهی از سرخ روئی بر سر
گهی اندر سماع شوق جانان　　شده بی پا وسر چون چرخ گر
بهر نغمه که از مطرب شنیده　　بدو وجدی از آن عالم ر
سماع جان نه آخر صوت و حرفست　　که در هر پرده سری شگرف
ز سر بیرون کشیده دلق ده توی[3]　　مجرد گشته از هر رنگ و هر ب
فرو شسته بدان صاف مروق　　همه رنگ سیاه و سبز و از
یکی پیمانه خورده از می صاف　　شده زان صوفیء صافی ز اوص
بجان خاک مزابل پاک رفته　　ز هر چه آن دیده از صد یک
گرفته دامن رندان خمار　　ز شیخی و مریدی گشته
چه[5] جای زهد و تقوی این چه قیدست　　چه شیخی و مریدی این چه شید
اگر روی تو باشد بر که و مه　　بت و زنار و ترسائی ت[6]

[1] L. گهی
[2] H. راز
[3] H. تو
[4] H. بو
[5] L. transposes the lines of this couplet.
[6] H. here repeats couplets 761 and 762.

١٥ سؤال

بت و زنار و ترسائی درین کوی　　همه کفرست وگرنه چیست بر

١٥ جواب

بت اینجا مظهر عشقست و وحدت　　بود زنار بستن عقد خد
چو کفر و دین بود قایم بهستی　　شود توحید عین بت ب

شیا هست هستی را مظاهر   از آن جمله یکی بت[1] باشد آخر

ندیشه کن ای مرد عاقل   که بت از روی هستی[2] نیست باطل

کایزد تعالی خالق اوست   ز نیکو هرچه صادر گشت نیکوست

انجا که باشد محض خیرست   اگر شری ست[3] در وی آن زغیرست

ن گر بدانستی که بت[4] چیست   بدانستی که دین در بت پرستیست

مشرک ز بت آگاه گشتی   کجا در دین خود گمراه گشتی

او در[5] بت الا خلق ظاهر   بدان علت شد اندر شرع کافر

گر زو نه بینی حق پنهان   بشرع اندر نخوانندت مسلمان

یح و نماز و ختم قران   نگردد هرگز این کافر مسلمان

سلام مجازی گشته بیزار   کرا کفر حقیقی شد پدیدار

ن هر تنی جانی است پنهان   بزیر کفر ایمانی است پنهان

کفر از تسبیح حق[7] ست   وان من شیء گفت اینجا چه دقست

لویم که دور افتادم از راه   فذرهم بعد ما جاءت قل الله

خوبی رخ بت را که آراست   که گشتی بت پرست ار[8] حق نمیخواست

کرد[9] هم او گفت وهم او بود   نکو[10] کرد[9] و[10] نکو[10] گفت و نکو[10] بود

بین و یکی گوی و یکی دان   بدین ختم[11] آمد اصل و فرع ایمان

ن میگویم این بشنو ز قرآن   تفاوت نیست اندر خلق رحمان

اشارت بزنار

ن خدمت آمد عقد زنار   نظر کردم بدیدم اصل هر کار

---

1 H. شد
2 H. معنی
3 H. شرست
4 H. دین
5 L. از
6 L. omits this couplet.
7 H. حق اوست
8 H. از
9 H. گردد
10 H. نیکو
11 H. اصل

نباشد اهل دانش را معوّل ز هر چیزی مگر بر وضعِ
میان دربند چون مردان بمردی درآ در زمرهٔ اوفوا بعه
برخش علم و چوگان عبادت ز میدان در ربا گوی سعا
ترا از بهر این کار آفریدند اگرچه خلق بسیار آفر
پدر چون علم وُ[1] مادر هست اعمال بسانِ قرّة آلعین است اح
نباشد بی پدر انسان شکی نیست مسیح اندر جهان بیش از یکی نیس
رها کن ترّهات و شطح و طامات خیال نور و اسباب کرا
کرامات تو اندر حق پرستیست[2] جز آن کبر و ریا و عجبِ هست
درین هر چیزکان نه زباب فقر ست همه اسباب استدراج و مکر
ز ابلیسِ لعینی[3] بی شهادت شود صادر[4] هزاران خرق[5] عا
که از دیوارت آید گاه از بام گهی در دل نشیند گه در
همی داند ز تو احوال پنهان درآرد در[6] تو فسق و کفر و[7] عص
شد ابلیست امام و در پس تو بدو لیکن بدینها کی رس
کرامات تو گر در خود نمائیست[8] تو فرعونی و این دعوی خدائیس
کسی کو راست باحق آشنائی نیاید هرگز از وی خود
همه روی تو در خلقست زینهار مکن خود را در[9] ین علّت گ
چو با عامه نشینی مسخ گردی چه جای مسخ یک ره فسخ[10] گ
مبادت هیچ با عامت سروکار که از فطرت شوی ناگه نگو
تلف کردی بهرزه نازنین عمر نگوئی در چه کار است اینچنین
بجمعیت لقب کردند تشویش خریرا پیشوا کرده زهی

[1] و omitted. H.
[2] مستیست H.
[3] لعین H.
[4] پیدا L.
[5] حرف H.
[6] در omitted. H.
[7] و omitted. H.
[8] نیست H.
[9] بد L.
[10] نسخ H.

ده سروری اکنون بجهّال — از ین گشتند مردم جمله بدحال
دجّال اعور تا چه گونه — فرستاده است در عالم نمونه
باز بین ای مرد حسّاس — خراورا دان[1] که نامش هست[2] جسّاس[3]
را این[4] همه هم[5] تنگ آن خر — شده از جهل پیش آهنگ آن خر
خواجه قصّهٔ آخر زمان کرد — بچندین جا ازین معنی نشان[6] کرد
ن اکنون که کور و کرشبان شد — علوم دین همه بر آسمان شد
ر اندر میانه رفق و آزرم — نمیدارد کسی از جاهلی شرم
احوال عالم بازگون است — اگر تو عاقلی بنگر که چون[7] است
ی کز باب لعن وطرد ومقتست[8] — پدر نیکو بد اکنون شیخ وقتست
ر میکشت آن فرزند طالح — که اورا بُد پدر با جدّ صالح
ن با شیخ خود کردی تو ای خر — خری را کز خری هست از تو خرتر
او لا یعرف الهرّا[9] من البرّ — چگونه پاک گرداند[10] ترا سرّ
ر دارد نشان باب خود پور — چگویم چون بود نورٌ علی نور
کو نیک رای و نیک بختست — چو میوه زبدهٔ سرّ[11] درختست
یکن شیخ دین کی گردد آنکو — نداند نیک از بد بد ز نیکو
دی علم دین آموختن بود — چراغ دین ز نور[12] افروختن بود
ی از مرده علم آموخت هرگز — ز خاکستر چراغ افروخت هرگز
در دل همی گردد[13] بدین کار — ببندم در میان خویش زنّار
آن معنی که من شهرت ندارم — بلی دارم ولی زان هست عارم[14]
یکم چون خسیس آمد درین کار — خمولم بهتر از شهرت[15] به بسیار

[1] دان omitted. H.
[2] گشت H.
[3] خباس ? L.
[4] بهن L.
[5] در L.
[6] بیان L.
[7] چه گونه H.
[8] دقت است H.
[9] أ omitted. H.
[10] کرده اند H.
[11] سرو H.
[12] جان H.
[13] همین آید هنر L.
[14] هیبت ندارم. H.
[15] H. adds او

دگر باره رسید الهامی از حق   که بر حکمت مگیر از ابلهی د
اگر کنّاسی نبود در ممالک   همه خلق اوفتند اندر مهالک
بود جنسیت آخر علت ضم   چنین آمد جهان و الله
و لیک از صحبت نا اهل بگریز   عبادت خواهی از عادت بپ
نگردد جمع عادت با عبادت   عبادت میکنی بگذر ز عاد

اشارت بترسائی

ز ترسائی فرض تجرید دیدم   خلاص از ربقهٔ تقلید د
جناب قدس وحدت دیر جانست   که سیمرغ بقارا آشیانس
ز روح الله پیدا گشت این کار   که از روح القدس آمد پد
هم از الله در پیش تو جانیست   که از روح القدس[1] در وی نشانیس
اگر یابی خلاص از نفس ناسوت   در آئی در حیات قدس لاهو
هر آنکس کو مجرّد چون ملک[2] شد   چو روح الله بر چارم فلک

تمثیل

بود محبوس طفل شیر خواره   بنزد مادر اندر گاه
چو گشت او بالغ و مرد سفر شد   اگر مردست همراه پدر
عناصر مر ترا چون ام سفلیست   تو فرزند و پدر آبای علویس
از ان گفتست عیسی گاه اسرا   که آهنگ پدر دارم ب
تو هم جان پدر سوی پدر شو   پدر رفتند همراهان پدر

[1] از قدوس الله در H.
[2] از چون شد H.

خواهی که گردی مرغ پرواز   جهان جیفه پیش کرکس انداز
ان ده مر این دنیای غدّار   که جز سگ را نشاید داد مُردار
ب چبود مناسب را طلب کن   بحقّ رو آور و ترک نسب کن
نیستی هرکو فرو شد   فلا انساب نقد وقتِ[1] او شد
ن نسبت که پیدا شد زشهوت   ندارد حاصلی جز کبر و نخوت
شهوت نبودی در میانه   نسبها جمله میگشتی فسانه
شهوت در میانه کارگر شد   یکی مادر شد آن دیگر پدر شد
م که مادر یا پدر کیست   که با ایشان بعزّت[2] بایدت زیست
ه ناقصی را نام خواهر   حسودی را لقب[3] کرده برادر
ن خویش را فرزند خوانی   ز خود بیگانه خویشاوند خوانی
ری بگو تا[4] خال و عمّ کیست   ازیشان حاصلی جز درد و غم چیست
نی[5] که با تو در طریقند   پیء هزل[6] ای برادر هم رفیقند
ن جدّ اگر یکدم[7] نشینی   ازیشان من چگویم تا چه بینی
فسانه و افسون و بندست[8]   بجان خواجه کاینها ریشخندست
ی وا رهان خودرا چو مردان   و لیکن حقّ کس ضایع مگردان
رع ار یک دقیقه ماند مهمل   شوی[9] در هر دو کون از دین معطّل
ن شرع را زنهار مگذار   و لیکن خویشتن را هم نگه دار
وزن[10] نیست الّا مایهء غم   بجا بگذار چون عیسیء مریم
فی شو ز هر قیدِ مذاهب   درآ در دیر دین مانند راهب
نا در نظر اغیار و غیرست   اگر در مسجدی آن عین دیرست

[1] L. حال
[2] L. بحرمت
[3] H. القب
[4] H. ما
[5] H. omits the ی
[6] H. منزل
[7] H. یکه سو
[8] H. پند
[9] L. شود
[10] L. زر و زن

چو برخیزد ز پیشت کسوت غیر   شود بهر تو مسجد صورت

نمیدانم بهر حالی که هستی   خلاف [1] نفس بیرون کن که ر

بت و زنّار و ترسائی و ناقوس   اشارت شد همه با ترک نام

اگر خواهی که گردی [2] بنده ٔ خاص   مهیّا شو برای صدق و اخلا

برو [3] خودرا ز راه خویش برگیر   بهر یک لحظه [4] ایمانی ز س

بباطن نفس تو چون هست کافر   مشو راضی بدین اسلام

ز تو هر لحظه ایمان تازه گردان   مسلمان شو مسلمان شو مس

بسی ایمان بود کز کفر زاید   نه کفرست آن کزو ایمان

ریا و سمعة و ناموس بگذار   بیفگن خرقه و بربند

چو پیر ما شو اندر کفر فردی   اگر مردی بده دل را

مجرّد شو ز هر اقرار و انکار   بترسازاده ده دل را ب

اشارت ببت و ترسابچه

بت و ترسابچه نوریست ظاهر   که از روی بتان دارد

کند او جمله دلهارا وثاقی [5]   گهی گردد مغنّی گاه

زهی مطرب که او از نغمه ٔ خوش   زند در خرمن صد زاهد

زهی ساقی که او از یک پیاله   کند بیخود دو صد هفتاد

اگر در مسجد آید در سحرگاه   بنگذارد در و یک مرد

رود در خانقه مست شبانه   کند افسون صوفی را

شود [6] در مدرسه چون مست مستور   فقیه از وی شود بیچاره

[1] H. inserts از
[2] H. کرده
[3] H. برد
[4] H. adds در
[5] H. وساقی
[6] H. رود

عشقش زاهدان بیچاره گشته | ز خان و مان خود آواره گشته
ی مؤمن دگررا کافر او کرد | همه عالم پر از شور و شر او کرد
ابات از لبش معمور گشته | مساجد از رخش پر نور گشته
کار من از وی شد میسّر | بدو دیدم خلاص از نفس کافر
م از دانش خود صد حجب داشت | ز عجب و نخوت و تلبیس[1] و پنداشت
آمد از درم آن بت سحرگاه | مرا از خواب غفلت کرد آگاه
رویش خلوت جان گشت روشن | بدو دیدم که تا خود چیستم من
کردم در رخ خوبش[2] نگاهی | برآمد از میان[3] جانم آهی
گفتا که ای شیّاد و سالوس | بسر شد عمرت اندر نام و ناموس
ین تا علم و زهد و کبر و پنداشت | ترا ای نارسیده از که وا داشت
ر کردن بروبم نیم ساعت | همی ارزد هزاران ساله طاعت
ی الجمله رخ آن عالم آرای | مرا با من نمود اندر سر و پای
ه شد روی جانم از خجالت | ز فوت عمر و ایّام بطالت
دید آن ماه کز روی چو خورشید | که ببریدم من از جان خود امّید
ی پیمانه پر کرد و بمن داد | که از آب وی آتش در من افتاد
ن گفت ازمی بی رنگ و بی بوی | نقوش تختهٔ هستی فرو شوی
آشامیدم آن پیمانه را[4] پاک | در افتادم ز مستی[5] بر سر خاک
ن نه نیستم در خود نه هستم | نه هشیارم نه مخمورم نه مستم
ی چون چشم او دارم سر خوش | گهی چون زلف او باشم در آتش[6]
ی از خوی خود در گلخنم من | گهی از روی او در گلشنم من

[1] ابلیس H.
[2] خویش H.
[3] بمان H.
[4] را omitted. H.
[5] هستی H.
[6] مشوّش L.

خاتمة

از آن گلشن گرفتم شمهٔ باز نهادم نام اورا گلشنِ راز

در و از رازها گلها شکفتست که تا اکنون کسی دیگر نگفتست

زبانِ سوسنِ او جمله گویاست عیونِ نرگسِ او جمله بیناست

تامّل کن بچشم دل یکایک که تا برخیزد از پیش تو این شک

به بین منقول و معقول و حقایق مصفّا کرده در علمِ دقائق

بچشم منکری منگر در و خوار که گلها گردد اندر چشم تو خار

نشانِ ناشناسی ناسپاسیست شناسای حق در حق شناسیست

غرض زین جمله آن تا گر کند یاد عزیزی گویدم رحمت بر و باد (MSS. تا گرما ،)

بنام خویش کردم ختم و پایان الهی عاقبت محمود گردان

تمّ الکتاب

بعون الملك الوهّاب

CPSIA information can be obtained at www.ICGtesting.com
Printed in the USA
LVOW06*1452020514

384226LV00004B/36/P

9 781164 709190